D1562866

CONTEMPLATIVE MASONRY

BASIC APPLICATIONS OF MINDFULNESS, MEDITATION, AND IMAGERY FOR THE CRAFT

REVISED & EXPANDED EDITION

C.R. DUNNING, JR.

Contemplative Masonry:
Basic Applications of Mindfulness, Meditation, and Imagery for the Craft
Revised & Expanded Edition

Published By:

Stone Guild Publishing
P.O. Box 250167
Plano, TX 75025-0167
http://www.stoneguildpublishing.com/

First Paperback Edition Published 2016

ISBN-13 978-1-60532-075-5
ISBN- 1-60532-075-7

10 9 8 7 6 5 4 3 2 1

ACKNOWLEDGMENTS

With deep gratitude, admiration, and respect, I wish to recognize the following people, all of whom have significantly influenced the writing of this book:

- Brother C.R. "Buddy" Dunning, Sr., may he rest in peace, for his fatherly example of what it means to be a brother Mason, and for leaving *Lightfoot's Manual of the Lodge* and *Morals and Dogma* out where his curious, young son could be captivated by their mysteries;

- John F. Miller, III, Ph.D., for treasured friendship, for mentoring in philosophy, and for being a great sage, scholar, and exemplar of love;

- M∴A∴, for encouraging authenticity and disciplined practice in my spirituality;

- T∴F∴S∴, for cherished companionship, for being a frequent source of inspiration and an example of reflective learning, holism, and compassionate presence;

- Brothers Bob Davis and Jim Tresner, for close comradeship, for sharing so many Masonic hopes, dreams, and visions, and for encouraging me to provide contemplative practice as a form of Masonic education;

- Brother Kevin Main, for dear friendship, enthusiasm for both the inner and outer work of Masonry, and for his invaluable assistance in editing and producing this edition of *Contemplative Masonry*;

- Brothers Matt Anthony, Jason Marshall, and Nathan Warren, staff of *The Laudable Pursuit* website and podcast, for warm friendship and their personal investment in contemplative practice and promotion of its value in Masonry;

- Lastly, and by no means least, Susan Dunning, beloved spouse, for providing invaluable encouragement and support for my passion and commitment in this work, and for modeling thoughtfulness manifested in productive action.

DEDICATION

Contemplative Masonry is dedicated to
the Great Architect of the Universe,
and to every Mason who asks, seeks, and knocks
to engage in transformative encounters with the Light.

Gnothi Seauton

Hoc Opus! Hic Labor Est!

TABLE OF CONTENTS

ILLUSTRATIONS

Note that alchemical illustrations have been chosen for many of the sections in this book. In general, psychospiritual alchemy has the same aims as contemplative Masonry. However, the originally intended significance of each emblem is not necessarily reflected in its respective section of this book.

FORWARD
BY JIM TRESNER, 33° G.C.

Dr. Robert Lee Jones, Professor of Comparative Religion at Oklahoma City University, with a degree in theology from the University at Edinburgh, was one of the most intelligent, highly educated, wise, and gentle men I have ever known. In the final lecture of his "Religions of Mankind" class, he was wont to say, "I would be very disappointed in any of you who went for a walk in the woods expecting to see an elf. I would be even more disappointed if you were surprised when you did see one."

He was trying to teach us the attitude—the mind-set—with which one should approach the fact that we are complex critters in a more complex world than we sometimes realize. My Father, also a highly intelligent, educated, wise, and gentle man, often put it like this: "Jim, if it looks like a duck, walks like a duck, and quacks like a duck, be very sure it isn't a walrus in deep disguise, and be very, very sure you would know the difference."

Chuck Dunning, one of my most favorite people—another highly intelligent, educated, wise, and gentle man—has written what might be called a "Hitchhiker's Guide to Reality," or, perhaps, a *vade mecum* for duck/walrus disambiguation. A highly-skilled counselor and therapist, he deals constantly with that most perplexing question, "What are we, really?"

For most of my lifetime, our culture, and even some theologians and psychologists, have tried to create and foster a mechanical sort of answer to that question, a stimulus/response definition of humanity. "Push this button, and out comes this response." Most theologians and psychologists, and almost everyone in the arts, have known that this simply isn't true. If we are machines, we operate with a large degree of chaos; and most of us, admit it or not, can relate to the cartoon which shows a complex mathematical formula on the chalkboard with a little note halfway through: "the magic happens here."

That disinclination to accept the existence of the spiritual nature in mankind became virtually culture-wide. It arose in Masonry, which was the last place one would have expected to see it. More than one Masonic leader has dismissed the entire spiritual, non-material aspect of Freemasonry as "that weird stuff," which was of interest only to loons and had nothing to do with Masonry (which consisted of charity, fish-fries, and memorizing the words of the ritual).

But there have been voices throughout time telling of the importance of the spiritual and man's participation in it.

John Calvin—hardly a wild-eyed liberal in theology—speaks of man's mystical participation in the Divine.

Albert Einstein is quoted as having said, "The intuitive mind is a sacred gift, and the rational mind is a faithful servant. We have created a society which honors the servant and has forgotten the gift."

Albert Pike, in the ritual of the 18th Degree of the Scottish Rite, tells us that the question of the spiritual connection of mankind with the Divine is the most important question there is, because the issue of whether man is of any more consequence than an ant depends on the answer. In another of his writings, he tells us that the human will is a force, in the same sense and way that gravity is a force or electricity is a force.

Native American teaching legends stress the interconnectedness of all things with the spirit of a person.

Professor Steven Bullock, author of *Revolutionary Brotherhood*, in both an interview on the History Channel and in the video-recorded lecture "Sensible Signs: The Emblematic Education of Post-Revolutionary Freemasonry," states that one of the accomplishments of early Freemasonry was to combine the rationality of the Enlightenment with the earlier mystical/spiritual/religious traditions.

And, as Brother Dunning so clearly demonstrates, the Degrees of the Blue Lodge are chock-full of references to the fact that man is a spiritual being with spiritual talents and abilities which can be awakened and developed.

This book is not a tour though the vague mists of Avalon. It is a practical, reasonable guide to development. In many ways it is like a video on muscular development. Follow the exercises, and you will see results. Leave it on the shelf, and nothing will happen.

But how? You are about to find out.

And if it is true that Masonry takes good men and makes them better, how does it do it? You are about to find out.

If it is true that the essence of Masonry is a quest to discover your own true nature, how do you make that discovery? You are about to find out.

If it is true that contemplation is a talent which can be grown and developed, how do you do it? You are about to find out.

If intuition is not just a vague hunch or a lucky guess, what is it? You are about to find out.

And if you are ever bothered in the still, small watches of the night by the question, "Who or what I am?", you will at least have a good chance of finding out.

You may even figure out what to do if you see an elf.

PREFACE

When *Contemplative Masonry* was first published as a down-loadable manuscript on MasterMason.com in 2000, it was the result of 12 years of fairly ordinary Masonic fraternal experience combined with contemplative practice. It was an effort to provide other Masons with what I'd hoped to encounter when I joined the fraternity in 1988. These ideas and practices were suggested by its own teaching, but I had instead been deeply disappointed to find them missing. While I managed within a couple of years to locate a few members with similar interests scattered around the USA, I hadn't located any systematic approach or guideline to contemplative practice in mainstream Masonry. Thankfully, this search was happening at the same time as the rise of the Internet, so that, by the late '90s, I was in frequent online communication with a few dozen Masons who not only shared my interests, but also encouraged the idea of developing a contemplative system for Masonry. Without that experience, I might've never written this book.

When the concept for the book arose and began to take shape, I believed it was best to publish it anonymously. There were various reasons for that belief, but I'm very happy to say things have changed. In fact, there are increasing numbers of good quality articles and books touching on the philosophical, psychological, and spiritual aspects of Masonry, and they are meeting with widespread acceptance. This development is interconnected with many more candidates coming to the fraternity with those very interests. The official leaders of the fraternity therefore increasingly recognize the importance of supporting these interests. With all of these developments, I've decided to reveal myself as the author of *Contemplative Masonry*. My intention is to join others in demonstrating that it's time for contemplative Masons to step forward and be openly recognized as such. We've come to a moment in Masonic history when we have the opportunity to assert that the wonderful allusions and promises of our ritual are not mere vanities, and that the initiatic mystery school we had hoped to find actually exists. By doing so, I hope the time soon arrives when every candidate who comes seeking for light in contemplative practice is welcomed with understanding and support.

Through many years of working with Masons and others on contemplative practice, one question that repeatedly arises is whether or not there is any particular concept of Deity contemplatives must hold or to which they are inevitably drawn by their practice. The short answer is no. Just as Masonry welcomes members of all faiths within its ranks, methods of contemplation are practiced by people from all faiths and with all sorts of beliefs about the Great Mystery, which we Masons address with such terms as "God," "Supreme Being," "Great Architect ," or "Deity." It is true that the traditional language of Masonry is monotheistic. We also typically speak of Deity in anthropomorphic terms, and I've largely adhered to that tradition in this book. I believe we should recognize that our tradition allows us, and sometimes even encourages us, to regard this language as an allegorical way of speaking about THAT which transcends language and is therefore ultimately ineffable. Interestingly, this perspective is shared by many of the greatest theologians of the monotheistic religions from which most of our ritual and symbolism is drawn. It might seem ironic, but appreciation of the ineffableness of Deity, combined with contemplative practice, tends to lead one into a greater awareness of one's own intimate relationship with Deity, as well as with our fellow human beings.

Were I to start writing *Contemplative Masonry* as a completely new book today, I am quite sure the result would be very different in significant ways; I have grown as a contemplative practitioner and, I hope, as a writer. In any case, my intention was, and continues to be, focused on inner work with themes traditionally presented in our rituals. It is important to note that the inner work is composed of "basic applications of mindfulness, meditation, and imagery." While the exercises provided do lay a solid foundation of inner work for the three Craft degrees, there are many other practices that can be done to receive further light in each of them. For instance, the very first exercise for the EA degree requires practicing mindfulness of the sensory experiences, but we have not followed up with a deeper contemplative penetration of the senses in the FC degree. Such work would be very fitting, because the FC degree draws our attention to the relationship between our senses and our under-standings of this world and our lives in it. This is but one example of how much potential remains for using our degrees as well-furnished workshops for contemplative labors. One day I might produce an-other volume to delve into some of those possibilities, but I think the collection of tools in this kit is sufficient. Even so, there is one major addition to the contemplative exercises offered in previous editions. The inner work for the Master Mason degree now includes an exer-cise that focuses on what I've come to know is such a central theme in Masonry that I'm almost ashamed to say I largely neglected it in the earlier editions. That theme is *love*! While love was directly touched upon in the last exercise of the older editions, it hardly received the attention it deserves. If Masonry is to make us truly better people, then what part of it is *not* aimed at helping us be more genuinely and completely loving? You'll also find the three chapters of the original text preceded by two chapters that are more conceptual in nature, the first providing a carefully structured look at the inherent psychology of our Craft, and the second elucidating how the Craft itself encour-ages and instructs us to engage in its deeper esoteric dimensions. These two chapters lay a more thorough intellectual foundation than was previously provided for the inner work.

It could be reasonably asked why I haven't included much in the way of historical analysis or argument to support the ideas and practices presented in this book. My first response is that I have no doubt such work is worthwhile, and I would welcome anyone doing so. In fact, there are some first-class Masonic historians who are very effectively making the case that our early Speculative brethren were very interested in the philosophical and spiritual potentials of the Craft. However, I am not a historical scholar, and there have already been too many Masonic authors who've made poor, misleading, and even blatantly false historical claims to defend their inspirations, musings, and speculations about our Craft. My approach is simply to take Masonry's inherited ritual and monitorial instructions as worthy of serious attention, consideration, and contemplation, and then share what happens when I do so. It's impossible for me to believe that our ancient brethren intended otherwise.

It is fitting to close with the disclaimer that the views presented in this book are based upon my own studies, practices, and insights; I neither speak for the fraternity as a whole, nor tell other Masons how they must understand or experience Masonry. With these things in mind, if you're reading this book because you're interested in new or different concepts about Masonry, then I hope you find something useful. However, I promise you'll get much more Masonic light by actually practicing the exercises provided in the last three chapters.

Fiat Lux!
C.R. "Chuck" Dunning, Jr.

"*Masonry, successor of the Mysteries, still follows the ancient manner of teaching. Her ceremonies are like the ancient mystic shows, —not the reading of an essay, but the opening of a problem, requiring research, and constituting philosophy the arch-expounder. Her symbols are the instruction she gives. The lectures are endeavors, often partial and one-sided, to interpret these symbols. He who would become an accomplished Mason must not be content merely to hear, or even to understand, the lectures; he must, aided by them, and they having, as it were, marked out the way for him, study, interpret, and develop these symbols for himself.*"

Albert Pike, Morals and Dogma

INTRODUCTION

Speculative Masonry is often referred to as a system of morality, veiled in allegory and illustrated by symbols. We are taught that by this Craft we learn to subdue our passions and improve ourselves as citizens, family members, and servants of our Creator. It is said that under the guidance of the Supreme Architect of the Universe, we may better display the virtues of truth, relief, and brotherly love. We learn that to progress as a Mason is to mature in wisdom, strength, and beauty. All of these things are the teachings of Speculative Masonry. But what is it that most fully reveals the light and life of our art, bringing those objectives to their greatest fruition? Our tradition tells us that Speculative Masonry "leads the contemplative to view with reverence and admiration the glorious works of creation, and inspires him with the most exalted ideas of the perfections of his Divine Creator." It should be recognized that this passage distinguishes the *contemplative* Mason as one who is guided by the Craft to be more reverent, admiring, and inspired than one might otherwise be.

A contemplative Mason is therefore more than an academic student of Masonry. It is easy for us to read the published works of Masonic authors who qualify as contemplatives; however, simply absorbing whatever light they may reveal does not make us contemplative Masons. A true contemplative uses the faculties of the psyche as a collection of fine working tools. One learns to employ those tools with the proper measures of force and precision in order to more fully reveal the wisdom, strength, and beauty in whatever matter is chosen. One thus makes of oneself a true philosopher, a literal "lover of wisdom."

You are now encouraged to take up your own tools and focus upon the raw materials supplied to you by your Creator and by the Craft. In doing so, you embark not only on a work that reveals greater meaning and depth in Masonry, but more importantly, you can ascend the steps of apprenticeship, craftsmanship, and mastery in your own life. *Indeed, a foundation stone of this book is the premise that psychological and spiritual maturation is perhaps the loftiest purpose of our art.* In this introduction, we will begin clarifying what it means to mature in this way. We will also begin to consider the working tools of the psyche and how they are employed.

HOLISTIC MATURATION

Holistic maturation is a developmental process that leads human beings to become more whole, integrated, healthy, and competent in all areas of life. In the broadest sense, such maturation is a psychological process. The psychology of our Craft will therefore be examined in further detail later in this book, and so for now, we will consider only a quick summary of its relevance to the contemplative work of holistic maturation. The science of psychology recognizes that we are beings with behaviors, emotions, and both conscious and unconscious mental processes. The psychological ideal is that these factors should work together in a coordinated and efficient manner. Religion has also recognized these levels of our being but has insisted that there are other levels beyond these, traditionally referring to such levels under the heading of spirit. As the territories of science and religion have become more intertwined, theologians have begun to realize that an understanding of psychology has a meaningful place in a life of faith and good works. Likewise, psychologists increasingly acknowledge that there is much wisdom in seeing human consciousness as intimately connected with levels of intelligence that transcend our normal awareness. In fact, both of these fields have always had much in common.

THE DESIGN UPON THE TRESTLE-BOARD

Humanity's great spiritual traditions have constructed models of the psyche that reflect a deep awareness of different dimensions to our being. Although the names, number, and arrangements of such dimensions vary, there does seem to be an underlying pattern that is common to all. For the sake of simplicity, and to avoid an over-identification with any single religious tradition, this book uses the following model for the basic structure of the human psyche:

Dimensions	Functions
Spiritual	intuition*, inspiration, wisdom, creativity, and will
Mental	cognition, reasoning, analysis, memory, imagination, innovation, judgment, and understanding
Emotional	desire, attraction, repulsion, pleasure, pain, fear, joy, compassion, and the infinite variety of our "feelings"
Physical	physiological processes, including our sensations of, and actions upon, the environment, other people, and ourselves

* Note: Throughout this book, the term "intuition" is used in a manner that is not as common as it perhaps once was. Today it is often used in reference to hunches, quickly drawn conclusions based upon superficial observations, or even knee-jerk reactions. By contrast, our use of the term addresses the deep unconscious or semiconscious processes that contribute to, and are often sensed immediately prior to, an insight or epiphany.

We conceptualize these dimensions arranged in a hierarchy as though rungs on a ladder or steps in a staircase. Reflecting upon the development of human beings, we can see that all of us naturally follow an upwardly spiraling course of expanding consciousness. As infants, our focus is physical. As toddlers, emotions begin demanding our attention. In the years of kindergarten and grade school, we begin to more directly explore the faculties and potentials of the mind. Eventually, we may even realize the need to consider a more mysterious and less tangible dimension of reality.

Our lives as infants are focused on mastering our physical being. Nature demands that our primary tasks are to eat, crawl, and walk. Our senses deliver information about our bodies and the world around us. We use that information so that our bodies may respond in a way that ensures our survival.

New levels of physical mastery lead us to the necessity for new levels of emotional awareness and control. Anyone who has witnessed the growth of a child knows that when the walking and talking start, so do the needs for emotional education and discipline. Without developing emotional awareness and responsibility, we are destined to become unstable, offensive, and even dangerous to others and to ourselves.

In trying to work out acceptable solutions to our physical and emotional problems, we encounter the faculties of the mind. In our imaginations, we see or feel the thing we desire. We imagine what sorts of behavior might be successful in acquiring the object of that desire. We become aware of the rules of language, learning to express what we desire and imagine, and to understand what others desire and imagine. We internalize that language and begin mentally speaking to ourselves. Thus we develop more efficient means to analyze, reason, and judge the validity of one idea over another. By the time most of us are in our early teens we have begun abstract reasoning.

For most of us this new level of inner awareness and ability to think leads to profound experiences and realizations. We discover that there are mysteries about our existence that cannot be fully illuminated by our senses, emotions, or thoughts. Absurdities and paradoxes in the conventional views of reality begin to make themselves apparent. We witness the production of beautiful works of art, yet are unable to explain exactly from where or how the inspirations have come. We become aware that sometimes we receive understanding and insights that do not appear to come directly from our own conscious thoughts. Some of us experience psychic phenomena. Many of us have mystical moments, knowing the presence of some awesome transcendent truth that cannot be adequately expressed. All of these experiences and realizations beg our attention and urge us to begin exploring the spiritual dimension of our being. As a later section of this book will show, Masonry frequently encourages us to engage this dimension as directly as possible.

CONTEMPLATIVE WORKING TOOLS

Most simply stated, the various functions of the psyche are the working tools of contemplative Masonry. As a contemplative Mason, you will explore new depths, purposes, and methods of operation for your senses, emotions, cognition, and intuition. You will apply these skills to gain a deeper understanding of the symbols, rituals, and teachings of Masonry. In so doing, you will also achieve a deeper understanding of yourself and your relationships with the world, other human beings, and your Creator.

PHYSICAL

As Speculative Masons, we are admonished to follow a path of moral discipline. At its most basic level, this is a physical task. We keep within the due bounds of good behavior by doing what is healthy, fair, and respectful, and avoiding what is unhealthy, unfair, and disrespectful. When we are active in a lodge or temple, we observe and participate in rituals. We see symbols, hear statements, and make body motions that continually remind us of our physical obligations to God, our country, our families, and to our fraternity. As a contemplative Mason, you can endeavor to experience these sensations as clearly as possible and act with greater awareness and sense of purpose.

EMOTIONAL

Our tradition teaches that it is virtuous to subdue our passions, but the word "subdue" can be misleading. We often think that to subdue something means to suppress or to eliminate it. However, in a Masonic context the word more properly refers to a degree of complete mastery. In order to master our passions we should not deny or suppress our feelings. Rather, we should develop an acute awareness of them. By doing so, we begin to appreciate their complexities. We learn that even undesirable emotions can be seen in a positive light when properly understood and managed. We find that emotions are a form of energy, and that they can be employed for constructive purposes. As a contemplative Mason, you can become increasingly familiar with your emotions and use them as tools to stimulate deeper insight and healthier behavior.

MENTAL

As Speculative Masons, we are taught to improve our minds and consciences, and that a study of the arts and sciences will polish and adorn our minds. Our rituals place candidates in a state of darkness, forcing them to use their imaginations. We are brought to light and shown symbols to ponder. Many jurisdictions preserve the ancient requirement of learning a Masonic catechism handed down by oral instruction. These questions and answers give us many opportunities to memorize and reflect upon the history, philosophy, and tenets of our order. We are taught that conduct, guided by reason and good judgment, is one of our goals. We learn that truth is one of our principal tenets, a theme to contemplate as we join the heart and tongue with integrity. As a contemplative Mason, you can develop the ability to clear and focus your mental faculties, just as a master architect uses his instruments to read and produce the plans for each detail of a strong and beautiful building.

SPIRITUAL

Before becoming a Speculative Mason, we must acknowledge a belief in Deity. From that point forward we invoke the aid and blessings of the Supreme Architect of the Universe in all our great undertakings. We maintain faith and hope in an eternal life. We look to the beauty and perfection of nature for inspiration and to the wisdom of the scriptures for guidance. We listen for the still, small voice in our hearts. We ask, seek, and knock so that we may be admitted into that place where we shall receive more light. As a contemplative Mason, you can open the door of your spirit, learn to invoke your intuition, and see within yourself that inner spark of the Divine, the source of your true will, wisdom, and understanding.

THE INNER WORK

The exercises of this book are patterned after the three degrees of Craft Masonry and closely follow the Webb rituals as given in *Duncan's Ritual of Freemasonry*. Of course, ritual and symbolism vary according to jurisdiction, so practitioners are encouraged to make appropriate adjustments to reflect their own rituals and monitors. The chapters of this book comprise a series of instructions and exercises that should be taken in sequence and practiced with the recommended frequency and duration. We humans can be incredibly impatient and undisciplined, accustomed to having instant gratification and receiving complete information at the click of a button, but the goal of contemplative Masonry is not simply to acquire interesting bits of information. Contemplative Masonry is a developmental process, and each step along the way is a goal that should be accomplished before we are properly prepared to take the next step. Operative Masons know that to build properly one must first lay a foundation, then erect walls, and finally raise a roof to have an edifice that is actually functional. Once these steps are taken, then the adornment of the building can take place. In keeping with this point, the author has avoided producing a book with detailed commentary on our symbols and how they might be understood aside from what is taught in our rituals and monitors. This text is written as a guide and workbook for those who wish to practice contemplative Masonry, and they may do the work to acquire or craft such adornments for themselves.

Although this book is written primarily for individuals, it could be worthwhile to join others in this work. Having a group of like-minded companions on a journey such as this can provide benefits to all. Mutual encouragement and the open sharing of thoughts and feelings can help to maintain each person's enthusiasm and commitment to the work, as well as to stimulate insights that might otherwise remain untapped. The group may establish a healthy pace that motivates steady progress among its members. There is also often a valuable balancing effect that comes from the different perspectives, strengths, and limitations of the individuals in the group. On the other hand, group work can have its pitfalls. Individuals may find that a group moves either too quickly or too slowly to match their own progress. Power struggles, egos, and extreme differences in abilities or desires can interfere with optimal function of the group. Strong personalities can begin to influence unintentionally what the group will consider valid results from the work. More passive personalities may begin to unquestioningly accept the views of others as their own. The group can also become distracted by too much attention being given to extracurricular activities and interests. Still, the benefits can often outweigh the risks, and opportunities for working through this book with others should be given due consideration. After all, Masonry is first and foremost a fraternity.

Some words should also be said about the inherent risks for any individual doing contemplative work. Although this work in itself does not have the power to make a person mentally ill or emotionally unstable, it does have the power to amplify certain functions of the psyche. If you are a person with at least an average degree of self-awareness, emotional stability, and mental health, then you have no harm to fear from this work. On the other hand, if you are prone to visual or auditory hallucinations, mania, drug addiction, alcoholism, or a mood disorder requiring treatment, then you should consult with a mental health professional before attempting to complete the exercises in this book. Under no circumstances should any of this work be done while intoxicated by alcohol or an illicit drug. In all cases, it is wise to have at least one other person who knows what you are doing and with whom you can discuss your work on a regular basis. Of course, there are certain aspects of this work that can be quite challenging, even if you are a reasonably stable and healthy person. If you take it seriously and commit yourself to work diligently, you will be led to ask some difficult questions. It isn't often easy to question the behaviors, feelings, thoughts, and beliefs with which we have grown comfortable. Responding to such questions with integrity and courage may force you to confront unsettling realizations about yourself, the world, or even the Divine. At such moments you should ask yourself this: "Do I really desire more light? Is it worth it?" If you continue to say yes to each question, then you should go on. If not, then listen to your own heart and mind and follow their lead.

Finally, one may ask why this book does not present a specific and well-established contemplative path, such as those practiced in Kabbalah, mystical Christianity, Vedanta, Taoism, Buddhism, Hermeticism, Sufism and so on. Although such paths may each be perfectly suited to various individuals in Masonry, we cannot, in good conscience, prescribe any of them as a path that all Masons may follow. Masonry teaches us to be tolerant and inclusive of all religious traditions and spiritual perspectives, and so the theories and exercises of this book are intended to be compatible with many forms of worship and faith. Upon completion of this book, you may continue working with its methods, or you may find that you have been led to another path of illumination. In any case, may brotherly love prevail, and every moral and social virtue cement us.

"On the mind all our knowledge must depend; what, therefore, can be a more proper subject for the investigation of Masons?"

**From the Fellow Craft
lecture on the five senses**

The Psychology of Masonry

Is Masonry actually and intentionally concerned with the psyches of its members? If it is, then there should be a coherent psychology communicated by our rituals and symbols. We can start answering that question by asking two further questions that should be familiar to every Entered Apprentice: Where were you first prepared to become a Mason? What did you come here to do?

As every Entered Apprentice learns, the *internal* qualities are what recommend one for Masonry. Where are those qualities if not in the psyche? Also, consider the speculative use of our working tools. In particular, the gavel teaches us to remove all vices and superfluities from our *minds and consciences*, and thus our psyches. The perfect ashlar is provided as an emblem of oneself made suitable for the Celestial Temple, which is a spiritual edifice. The point within the circle also alludes to the psyche in that it is said to represent the individual Mason and the circumscription of his *passions and prejudices*. Similarly, the four cardinal and three theological virtues address not only proper behaviors with others, but are primarily concerned with teaching us about the patterns of *thinking and attitudes* that are the internal, or psychological, prerequisites for the external behaviors of right living.

We could go on drawing examples from other degrees, but for now, it suffices to observe that all the social and moral virtues of the ideal Mason can only manifest through a properly prepared instrument, and that instrument is the psyche. Thus, the perspective taken in this book is that the well-being and improvement of the psyche is not only a matter of concern within Masonry, it is the *core issue*.

Before proceeding with an examination of the psychology of Masonry, we should first clarify what is meant by the word "psychology." Psychology literally means the study or science of the psyche, and *psyche* is a Greek word meaning "soul." Thus, we can rightly think of psychology as the study or science of the soul. It provides ways of engaging one's inner world and social relationships, just as the other sciences provide ways of engaging the physical world around us. In modern science, psychology includes the study of individual behavior, emotions, thinking, the nature and influence of the unconscious, psychosocial development, and psychotherapy, which is healing of the psyche. As we shall see, Masonry provides instruction and experience in each of these areas.

MASONRY'S UNDERSTANDING OF THE PSYCHE

To say that Masonry has a psychology is to say that it has within it either implicit or explicit answers to the following questions:

- What are the structure and dynamics of the psyche? In other words, what are the parts of the psyche, and how do they work with each other?
- What are the necessary conditions of a healthy psyche, and what is the basic nature of psychological illness? What is required for an ailing psyche to heal?
- How does the psyche naturally grow and acquire the characteristics of adulthood? How can the psyche develop in desirable ways?
- How do the interactions between psyches affect the individual psyche? What are the ideal conditions of relationships?

STRUCTURE AND DYNAMICS

We begin answering those questions by elucidating Masonry's view of the psyche's structure and dynamics. The ritual and lectures of Masonry directly address four different yet intertwining dimensions of the psyche, which were noted in the introduction to this book. First, we note that our tradition speaks of, and actually involves, the physical body and its behaviors. Second, it repeatedly touches on the emotions, passions, and desires. Third, it provides much instruction and stimulation for the intellect. Fourth, it reveres and nurtures the eternal spirit and free will.

The dynamics of the psyche are the ways these four dimensions – physical, emotional, intellectual and spiritual – interact with and affect each other. The teachings of Masonry make it clear there is a kind of hierarchy of functions within the psyche, an order in which one part can be largely ruled or managed by those above it. Masonry acknowledges that the body can easily be ruled by one's passions and desires. Yet we are also taught that the intellect, by concentrating on the principles of moral and social virtue, has the necessary tools and much power to circumscribe desires and keep passions within due bounds, thus giving us the potential to align our behavior more toward reason than toward emotion. The intellect, in turn, responds to the drive of free will and the callings of spirit.

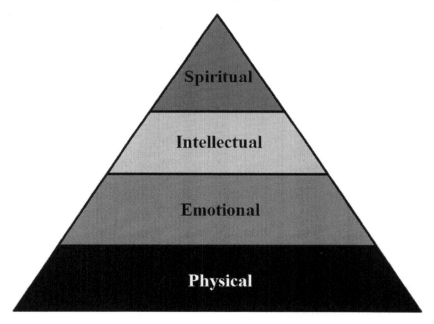

In short, spirit is at the top of the hierarchy, followed by the thinking mind, our feelings and emotions, and finally, our body and its actions. This order relates well with the Hierarchy of Needs proposed by the founder of humanistic psychology, Abraham Maslow. It is also closely related to the dynamics of transpersonal psychological theories such as those of Michael Washburn and Ken Wilber.

Within Masonry, there is also an implicit awareness of the unconscious dimensions of the psyche's structure and dynamics. Wherever Masonry speaks of mysteries, secrets, or darkness, it alludes to that which is hidden or unknown. That which is hidden or unknown about oneself is drawn forth in self-discovery from a region of the psyche that psychologists and therapists refer to as the *unconscious mind*, or simply the *unconscious*.

We differentiate the concept of the *sub*-conscious from the concept of the *un*-conscious by pointing out that the term "subconscious" implies an inferior position to the conscious mind. "Unconscious" denotes everything that is not only beneath the conscious mind but also all that is outside of it, parallel to it, and even beyond it. Like the conscious mind, the unconscious spans the physical, emotional, mental, and spiritual dimensions of being. We actually experience something emerging from the unconscious every time we dream, have a sudden intuitive insight or artistic inspiration, or find ourselves feeling or behaving in some surprising way.

Acknowledging the existence of the unconscious mind brings with it a responsibility to engage it as part of holistic maturation. As we shall see, the unconscious is actively engaged by Masonry, but if that connection is to be more fully comprehended, then the structure and dynamics of the unconscious should also be understood. The problem, of course, is that the unconscious is, so to speak, "a place of darkness." We cannot directly observe it as we do the other dimensions of the psyche but can only deduce things about it from the effects it has upon the conscious dimensions of the psyche. Thankfully, there are specialists in the psychology of the unconscious who have gone a long way in charting some of that "undiscovered country."

In the late 19th and early 20th centuries, pioneering psychologists like Sigmund Freud, Carl Jung, Alfred Adler, Otto Rank, and Robert Assagioli began to seriously study the unconscious and work with it in psychotherapy. Collectively, they and their followers are referred to as *depth psychologists*. These pioneers and others following in their footsteps, made great strides in exploring the relationship between the conscious and unconscious. Some of them realized that when contemplating a symbol and speculating upon its meaning, one can receive understanding and insights that seem to come out of nowhere, or even a vague sense of deeper meaning that urges further contemplation. Such experiences are evidence that some rumination and reflection occur on a level of mind not directly overseen and controlled in conscious awareness. These depth psychologists further discovered that symbols, whether visual images or characters of myth and legend, have the power to stimulate remarkably similar insights and developmental experiences in persons who are separated by time, place, and culture. In other words, symbols connect us with things that have not merely been programmed into us by our environments. As an example relevant to Masonic symbolism, consider that the ancient Chinese sages Confucius and Mencius revered the square and compasses as representative of virtue and wisdom, and did so more than twenty centuries prior to the formation of the Grand Lodge of England!

What are those unconscious "things" that symbols tap into? Many depth psychologists refer to them as *archetypes* (literally "principal forms"), and they conclude that the unconscious must be something that transcends the individual consciousness and is a realm that holds these basic principles and powers of consciousness. Various analogies can be made to help explain what an archetype is and how it works. To some extent, an archetype is like a seed that lies hidden and unknown beneath the surface of the soil. When conditions are right for it to sprout into the light, the potentials within that seed manifest, producing a plant that is typical of its species yet unique in its particular being. In much the same way, an archetype lies hidden outside our conscious awareness, yet it can give rise to the flowering of certain patterns of thought and behavior in one human being that are essentially the same as would arise for another. We can also think of the connection between an archetype and our psyches as similar to the relationship of a gene to the formation of our physicality. Just as each gene stimulates the development of certain physical traits and tendencies, each archetype stimulates the development of certain psychological traits and tendencies.

Early depth psychologists were not the first persons to come upon such an idea. Several hundred years before them, Kabbalists were receiving similar insights about the *sephirot*, or the fundamental cosmic principles inherent in creation. We can go all the way back to Plato, who held that everything is manifested from a level of being wherein reside the purest ideal forms of all that can possibly exist. Prior to Plato, we find a concept of archetypes expounded by Masonry's old friend, Pythagoras. Pythagoras said that numbers are the foundations of everything. Each number was understood to have its own peculiar nature and potentials, and to be godlike in its power to manifest certain things in this world. Many centuries later, at about the same time depth psychology gave us a theory of psychological archetypes, Kurt Gödel, one of the most stunning mathematical minds in history, also concluded that numbers are not merely quantities derived from observing things in the physical world. Gödel, echoing Pythagoras, conceived of numbers as principles transcending the processes of sense perception and logic, and therefore beyond complete comprehension; in effect, numbers are archetypes and numerals are the symbols that represent them.

More than one Masonic scholar has noted the importance of numeric symbolism in Masonry, and the ritual itself draws our attention to the art of arithmetic, "by which we learn the properties of numbers." Indeed, many versions of ritual openly declare that Masonry is identical with geometry. Our most revered working tools and the very emblems of our tradition itself, the square and compasses, are geometrical instruments. They are employed in making operative connections between the physical world and the world of numbers; just as for Speculative Masons they make connections between the world of moral ideals and our social behavior. So it is that we come back to Masonry's view of the psyche and its innate awareness that symbolism is the means by which the archetypes hidden within the unconscious can shed more light on our conscious lives.

HEALTH AND DISEASE

We now turn our attention to the matters of psychological health and disease. The concept of health in Masonry is fairly simple and straightforward, and is repeatedly indicated by our symbols and teachings. We can begin to understand the Masonic concept of health by considering the ideal conditions in a lodge – peace, harmony and unity – and that these conditions should be a reflection of the hearts and minds of its members. Here again we are reminded of Masonry's holism. In the Ancient and Accepted Scottish Rite, this ideal is summed up in a single word – *equilibrium*. Psychologically speaking, it is the harmonious integration of our physical, emotional, intellectual, and spiritual dimensions. Yet such a condition should not be mistaken as a static balance, for human beings are constantly experiencing change, both within us and around us.

Just as establishing and maintaining peace, harmony, and unity in a lodge requires constant attention and effort, so it is in the individual psyche. Our ritual teaches that this work requires three principle supports to the lodge – Wisdom, Strength, and Beauty – and therefore we should apply them to our own internal well-being. Beauty speaks of the proper proportions, gracefulness, and uniqueness that make an edifice, or a human being, admirable and pleasant to experience. Strength speaks of the durability of something, as well as its power to affect other things. Thus a healthy psyche is both resilient in the face of change and effective in accomplishing beneficial change. Wisdom speaks of the knowledge and skills required to stimulate, accept, and adjust to change in ways that establish and maintain both beauty and strength.

If health is Masonically understood as equilibrium, then disease is imbalance or disharmony among our physical, emotional, intellectual, and spiritual dimensions. Where psychological health is characterized by an inner peace and harmony that is composed of wisdom, strength, and beauty, psychological disease and disharmony is characterized by an inability or failure to accept and adjust to change in ways that establish and maintain both beauty and strength. Healing of any psychological infirmity should therefore knowingly and willingly engage change in just that way. We should come to understand how it is that we have been lacking in wisdom, strength, and beauty; envision what we wish to attain; appreciate and maximize our natural assets, talents, and potentials; acquire the support and other resources we need; and act on clear and reasonable goals and objectives for beneficial change.

It should also be noted that a social dimension of one's psychological health and healing is at least implicit within Masonry. All our lessons about relief and our obligations about helping, aiding, and assisting each other cannot be limited to our physical and financial wellbeing. Surely there isn't a Mason alive who doesn't want and need something more than that from the charitable hand of friendship and the welcoming arms of brotherly love. Consider, as only one example, the value to our mental and emotional wellbeing in seeking, offering, and listening to instruction and good counsel among each other.

MATURATION AND DEVELOPMENT

Our ritual provides a specific vision for developing the desirable conditions of adulthood:

> *"In youth, as Entered Apprentices, we ought industriously to occupy our minds in the attainment of useful knowledge; in manhood, as Fellow Crafts, we should apply our knowledge to the discharge of our respective duties to God, our neighbors, and ourselves; so that in old age, as Master Masons, we may enjoy the happy reflections consequent on a well-spent life, and die in the hope of a glorious immortality."*

Clearly, Masonry does not assume that the physical aging process itself naturally fulfills the ideals of wisdom, strength, and beauty in a well-balanced and holistically mature psyche. Time alone does not deliver us from "the numerous evils incident to childhood and youth" so that we can, with "health and vigor arrive at the years of manhood." One of the most significant principles within this teaching is that healthy holistic maturation requires intentional and purposeful effort, first in becoming educated about the various dimensions of our being, and then in applying our knowledge and skills. With an ongoing commitment to learning and applying such knowledge, we can continually develop into wiser, stronger, and more beautiful human beings, more at peace and in harmony within ourselves and with the world around us. This Masonic path of developing toward the ideal of a truly adult psyche is communicated in many ways, but perhaps most clearly and specifically by referring to the cardinal and theological virtues – prudence, fortitude, temperance, justice, faith, hope and charity (or love) – which are ritually explained in terms of internal thoughts and feelings as well as external behaviors and relationships with others.

Again, it is stressed that knowledge and understanding alone are only the beginning, for we should also employ that knowledge with diligent efforts to accomplish actual development. To begin such work with conscious intent is the very meaning of the word "initiation." In Masonry, such transformations can occur across the entire range of human experience; they are therefore holistic, with different kinds of initiation involving development of the various dimensions of the psyche in different ways. We will consider these developments under four categories of initiation: *social, academic, philosophical*, and *spiritual*.

Social initiation is the most basic and universal level of Masonic initiatory development; it engages the psyche of the individual primarily in the physical and emotional dimensions, although mental faculties are certainly called upon in their support, and it is very likely to be guided by deep spiritual principles. At the very least, social initiation is the beginning of one's membership in the fraternity. New relationships with new responsibilities are begun, such as keeping the specific points of the obligations, the payment of dues, etc. New voluntary duties to the group may also be accepted, such as the holding of offices, serving on committees, or performing in rituals.

Masonic social initiation also includes the goal of development in the individual's moral life. The brunt of our ritual instruction and symbolism directly addresses this point, and almost every Mason should be able to find at least one other Mason qualified to serve as a mentor in moral and social virtues. The lessons and examples received in the lodge also encourage the social initiate of Masonry to have a positive attitude and beneficial presence in all relationships outside the lodge.

In the context of social initiation, Masonic rituals can also be *rites of passage*. A rite of passage is a significant developmental event in one's life, a milestone that indicates the individual has passed to a new level of cultural maturation, such as a first date, high school graduation, or marriage. Masonic ritual becomes a rite of passage when one considers it a landmark of adulthood, an entry into a circle of admired elders, or a deeper participation in the traditions of one's family or community.

An *academic initiation* may also occur. Academic initiation primarily involves the conscious mental dimension, although it will likely include concepts that address the other dimensions of being. Our tradition provides opportunities for such initiation by continually urging us to seek more light in studies beyond the ritual itself. Academic initiation has occurred when the individual becomes engaged in the following ways:

- repeatedly musing upon possible meanings of the elements of ritual;
- continually engaging in serious study to learn about various aspects of our rituals and about what others have discovered in them;
- consistently integrating these ideas into an increasingly comprehensive understanding of Masonry.

Academic initiation reaches beyond the fraternity as one finds great joy in exploring the fantastic wealth of knowledge that humanity has acquired across the eons of history. Such information makes the experience of our present life and times richer and more meaningful. The academic initiate often finds that one or a few closely related fields are of special interest, yet also gains a deeper appreciation for the interconnectedness of all fields of knowledge.

An academic initiation may also lead to or be part of a *philosophical initiation*. Philosophical initiation has occurred when one's desires and efforts are not simply for the pleasure of gaining more information. The word "philosophy" is composed of the Greek roots *philos* for love and *sophia* for wisdom, and thus it is literally the *love of wisdom*. A philosophical initiate therefore aims at a deeper understanding of self and our fellow human beings, and seeks to transform that understanding into wisdom. Almost anyone will learn and grow from Masonic experience, and thus be psychologically healed and transformed to some extent, even if that experience is primarily a social initiation. Yet, either because they come into the fraternity seeking deeper work, or because their Masonic experiences awaken them to such possibilities, some members intentionally engage themselves with Masonry for philosophical initiation. Those Masons consciously seek wisdom for their health and the transformation of their lives, and to become instruments of health and transformation for others.

Processes that aid such transformation of the psyche include more than just ritual, social involvement and academic pursuits. In both spiritual and therapeutic practice, transformation is powerfully facilitated by internal disciplines such as prayer, contemplation, meditation, active imagination, breathwork, and dreamwork. It should therefore be no surprise that Masonic ritual explicitly encourages the practice of prayer and contemplation. For example, we are taught to seek the blessings of Deity "before all great and noble undertakings," and we refer to the Volume of Sacred Law as our "rule and guide."

If Masonry had no concept of spirit as an inseparable dimension of the psyche, then there would be little need for these admonitions. We are also taught that Masonry "leads the *contemplative* to view with reverence and admiration the glorious works of creation, and inspires him with the most exalted ideas of the perfections of his Divine Creator." To open our souls in prayer and in contemplation of scripture, nature, and God is to acknowledge the limitations of ordinary consciousness and to welcome the possibility of inspiration, and perhaps even intervention, to ensure that our understandings and labors are in harmony with the designs of the Great Architect of the Universe.

In probing these mysteries, yet another sort of initiation and transformation may occur – *spiritual initiation*. Spiritual initiation is an awakening to a mysterious dimension of one's being that transcends, yet unifies, the physical, emotional and intellectual dimensions of psyche; it is thus the most holistic form of initiation. The developments induced through spiritual initiation are always about the individual becoming illuminated as a more inspired, loving, and effective instrument of the Divine, and thus a better servant of humanity. In short, spiritual initiation is the internal shift that has led some individuals to become humanity's greatest theologians, prophets, mystics, saints, and initiators.

The spiritual initiate does not make Masonry a religion as "religion" is commonly understood. Rather, Masonry becomes an intentional part of one's spiritual life and stirs the psyche to plumb the depths of the religion one considers one's own, while also remaining open to the wisdom, strengths, and beauties of others. So it is that a spiritual initiate is motivated not only to be immersed in the symbolism of Masonry, but also willingly draws its symbols deep within the psyche. One concentrates upon them and welcomes them to serve as archetypal keys to unlocking the mysteries of the unconscious and of the spirit.

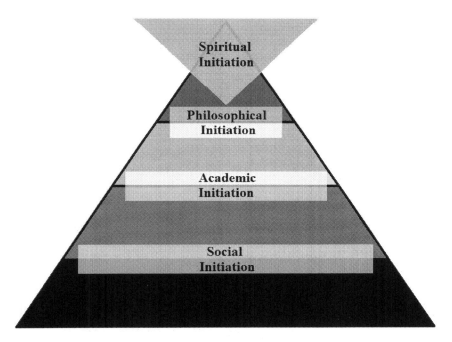

Because the spiritual dimension of the psyche unifies the other dimensions, the spiritual initiate is also a social, academic, and philosophical initiate, and is therefore most completely engaged in the work of holistic maturation. As a social initiate, one gladly opens the arms of brotherly love for people of other faiths. As an academic initi-ate, there is joy in learning more about the histories, myths, customs, and beliefs of different traditions. In this process one may come to see how various philosophies and religions express many of the same underlying truths, while also appreciating the uniqueness and special value held by each. As a philosophical initiate, one seeks ways that all of this knowledge and understanding can be integrated and applied for the advancement of peace, harmony, and unity within the rich diversity of all God's children. In summary, the spiritual initiate of Masonry understands and warmly embraces a duty to develop as a spiritual sibling to all fellow human beings.

RELATIONSHIPS

As we have clarified our tradition's basic understanding of the psyche's structure, dynamics, health, and maturation, we have already begun to see how relationships are essential to the fulfillment of Masonry's psychological potentials. We are now ready to more directly attend to what our tradition suggests about the psychology of relationships themselves.

To begin, consider that to be a Mason is to be part of a group that labors together toward common goals. Our rituals are thus filled with allegorical lessons about how people can and do cooperate with each other for their mutual benefit. In many Masonic jurisdictions, important aspects of our ideals about relationships are addressed after the new Entered Apprentice is brought to light and led to the northeast corner of the lodge. In the first degree we also learn of the principal tenets of Truth, Relief, and Brotherly Love, which describe the ideal ways that we should relate to each other. Our tradition also admonishes us to be good spouses, parents, and neighbors, and that we should avoid excesses that would be injurious to others. It reminds us that all people have a claim to our good will and caring service. It is also most telling that Masonry hardly ever speaks of the internal health and well-being of the individual without simultaneously addressing the individual's relationships with others. Masonry undeniably considers the individual and society as interconnected, each affecting the other in numerous ways, for better or worse.

As we have already seen, peace, harmony, unity, and all the wisdom, strengths, and beauties that produce and maintain those conditions, are taken as the broadly stated ideals for both the lodge and the individual psyche, and thus they become the ideals for all our relationships. Yet we should examine more closely how these ideals are actually exemplified in common Masonic fraternal relationships. As a graphic representing the field of Masonic relationships, consider three overlapping or interlocking circles in a triangular form. One of the circles represents the *Membership* aspect of Masonry, another represents *Instruction*, and the last circle represents *Initiation*. The area where all three circles overlap represents *Ritual*. Ritual is thus highlighted as the hub in which Masonic fraternal relationships are most clearly established and exemplified.

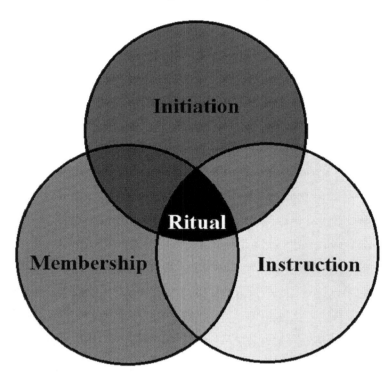

Ritual serves as the primary meeting place and central means of communication for these three general and interrelated aspects of the Masonic experience. Without ritual, some aspects of Masonic relationships could be established, but not as effectively. As illustrated by this image, all three areas include more than the elements and events of ritual itself. Each of these three aspects of Masonic relationships has much of its own territory outside of ritual, and they interact with each other outside of ritual, yet ritual brings all three together in a most powerful way.

To gain a deeper appreciation of what these three areas reveal about the psychology of relationships, we shall examine how they are specifically relevant to three aspects of one of the most intimate, respectful, and beneficial forms of human relationship, which is mentoring. In short, good Masonic mentors act in ways that support one's experience in all three of these areas, and thus provide examples for our own best behavior in relationships in and out of the lodge. In the following paragraphs we will examine each in more detail.

MEMBERSHIP

The psychological significance of membership is belonging, which addresses our most basic needs as social creatures. Our ritual is the means by which an individual cements a commitment to belong to the fraternity, and it also demonstrates the fraternity's welcoming and recognition of the individual. Much like a marriage ceremony, Masonic ritual provides a framework for entering into mutual obligations. Indeed, our tradition holds that it is the obligation that actually makes one a Mason. Belonging is thus established by the members' promises to support each other and to support family members as well. The Masonic experience amplifies this sense of belonging by clearly communicating mutual respect between the individual and the fraternity. The fraternity communicates its respect by maintaining the safety and dignity of the individual, while also providing sincere and reverent ceremonies that permit access to its most treasured secrets and benefits. The individual communicates respect by trusting the fraternity and submitting to the same tests, trials, and instructions as did those members who came before. If nothing else, this shared experience of ritual provides an instant point of contact and commonality among people who otherwise might never have come to know and enjoy each other's company. Outside of ritual, members can build on their sense of belonging and mutual respect by coming together for meals, attending to the business of maintaining an organization, and working together on social, academic, and philanthropic projects. In effect, the fraternity forms a kind of extended family, while also teaching that all of humanity should be considered a family, and every individual respected as a child of God.

In mentoring, the area of membership corresponds most directly to the role of companion. At the most basic level, a companion is someone who is simply present, and thus can be anyone with whom we share an experience or spend time. As good companions, mentors know when and how to listen, and how to find ways to personally relate to the experiences of others. Strong companions also share a sense of loyalty and commitment, a bond of trust, and a willingness to take on some portion of each other's burdens. Just as Masonic tradition ensures the immediate presence of a companion in almost every moment of ritual, so the fraternity ensures that every member has the opportunity to experience companionship outside of ritual. The mere presence of a genuinely engaged companion gives us strength, courage, and hope, conditions that Masonry urges us to foster in our relationships with all human beings.

INSTRUCTION

It is through instruction that Masonry directly addresses our higher emotional and intellectual needs for *understanding*, and the psychological processes of symbolism are intentionally engaged to that end. The experience of ritual provides instruction in the images, allegories, and myths that touch upon the archetypes of the unconscious and communicate our shared values, principles, and ideals. All cooperative relationships, including mentoring, should have a mutual understanding based on shared values, principles, and ideals, for without them, there is less shared identity, cohesion, or sense of direction and purpose. Without these points of connection, there is little real meaning in belonging, and therefore, ritual provides us with a reverent and dynamic process to help establish the meaning of our relationships.

The general purposes of instruction are to impart information and to encourage the search for knowledge and the plumbing of its depths, all with the aim of making life healthier, richer, and more pleasant for others as well as oneself. The *teacher* is therefore the mentoring role that corresponds to instruction. The teacher can be anyone who communicates information about Masonry, but it is especially the teacher's role to help one understand the information. Little needs to be said about the high priority Masonry places on education in our lodges and temples as well as in society. By including opportunities to experience mentors who act as truly caring teachers of our tradition and to develop one's own ability to teach, the Masonic experience provides a training ground that can help prepare its members for instructional roles in society, such as parenting, supervising or training others at work, or simply in helping friends and family learn from the experiences of everyday life.

What does the experience of Masonry reveal about how to teach effectively? Much of the power of ritual instruction lies in the fact that it is holistic, addressing and involving the whole range of human experience and expression – physical, emotional, mental, and spiritual. Because it is holistic, it is experiential, which means that its instructions are not merely provided as written or spoken information. Instruction is also experienced through visual signs and emblems, seeing and feeling physical objects, going through various bodily motions and movements about the room, hearing sounds such as gavel raps and music, sensing and reflecting the attitudes and emotions of the other members involved, and participating in moments of silence and prayer. Because ritual instruction is holistic and experiential, the mind is automatically engaged in forming concrete memories in connection with the symbolic images, attitudes, and ideas being communicated, which in turn make the recall of that information easier and more complete. Because it is holistic, experiential, and symbolic, it taps the unconscious mind more powerfully, which in turn, urges the conscious mind to find instruction outside the ritual from Masons and other resources, and to speculate and discover meanings that are beyond literal, and even moral, interpretations. Finally, ritual instruction demonstrates respect for its aims by maintaining traditional forms with artistic beauty and spiritual reverence. In this way we not only instruct the individual in specific lessons about moral and social virtues, but also simultaneously emphasize their intrinsic importance and value. In our lives beyond the ritual, both in and out of the lodge, we do well to give similar respect to anything of great significance that is being communicated to or by us. To carry these principles into our broader lives is to live as if every relationship, even life itself, is a kind of ritual of instruction in which every moment has the potential to reveal and communicate something of deep significance.

INITIATION

The initiatory aspect of our ritual separates Masonry from many other fraternal or social organizations. This distinction arises because Masonic ritual is more than induction into a group and instruction in its aims. As we have seen, Masonic initiations are symbolically, if not actually, turning points in a member's psychological development and holistic maturation – the Entered Apprentice as the ambitious youth, the Fellow Craft as the competent adult, and the Master Mason as the wise elder. Corresponding to transformations in different dimensions of the psyche, we have also seen different categories of initiation – social, academic, philosophical, and spiritual. Thus ceremonial initiation is the aspect of Masonic relationships that is about facilitating and celebrating a member's engagement in new efforts toward development and *transformation*.

With regard to mentoring, this area obviously relates most clearly to the role of the *initiator*, ritually illustrated by the Master of the lodge, who facilitates the transition and marks the progress of the individual Mason entering new phases of development. Outside of ritual, an initiator is typically an elder who has already successfully passed through the developmental transformations being approached by a less experienced person. A mentor acting as an initiator should therefore be a role model or exemplar who is legitimately entitled to challenge and welcome others into a specific social, psychological, or spiritual domain. Accepting the duty of being an authentic initiator means understanding that others, and especially those with less experience, will reflect our actions and attitudes to some extent; we should therefore willingly bear the responsibility to lead by example. The Master of the lodge also presents the candidate with tests and trials that, at least symbolically, require a demonstration of readiness and commitment to advance. Outside the lodge, we function as initiators in other pursuits by upholding the prerequisites and accomplishments necessary for others to be recognized as a peer or colleague in a given domain. Such practices are important in our relationships, because they help ensure mutual respect among persons with shared goals, as well as excellence and collective progress within a specific field of interest. For example, without appropriate scientific and professional standards, consider how little social prestige, quality in practice, or progress in learning there would be for the fields of architecture or medicine. Families, neighborhoods, and even nations have similar needs for standards and for mentors acting as initiators to uphold them.

SUMMARY

There can be no doubt that a comprehensive and functional psychology is inherent to Masonry. We have seen that our tradition provides us with profound clues and useful information about the structure, dynamics, and health of the psyche, as well as guidelines for holistic maturation and rich, rewarding relationships. All of this has been to expand upon the realization that Masonry's greatest purpose is to assist its members in transforming their lives into wiser, stronger, and more beautiful reflections of the Great Architect's designs for the human soul and society.

"It is for each individual Mason to discover the secret of Masonry, by reflection upon its symbols and a wise consideration and analysis of what is said and done in the work. Masonry does not inculcate her truths. She states them, once and briefly; or hints them, perhaps, darkly; or interposes a cloud between them and eyes that would be dazzled by them. 'Seek, and ye shall find,' knowledge and the truth."

Albert Pike, *Morals and Dogma*

A Straightforward Approach to Masonic Esotericism

Note: This chapter is based on an essay written for The Emerald Tablet, a publication of San Marcos Lodge #342 in San Marcos, Texas. It references the Preston/Webb family of ritual in Masonry, and most specifically that of the Grand Lodge of Texas, A.F. & A.M. Some details may therefore seem somewhat parochial. However, given the consistency of Masonry's teachings across jurisdictional and ritualistic lines, it is believed the observations, arguments, and conclusions of this article should be applicable to any experience of regular Craft Masonry.

Over the last decade, there has been a veritable explosion of discussion and writing about Masonic esotericism or esoteric Masonry, and much of it pertains to the same basic interests as those we are pursuing in contemplative Masonry. In many Masonic jurisdictions, it is customary to use the term "esoteric" to denote the parts of our work that are officially secret, those things that are not monitorial and are only performed in a tiled lodge or communicated between members. However, "esoteric" and "secret" are not entirely synonymous. The basic meaning of "esoteric" more broadly references the inner (*eso-*) nature of things, or the actualities and potentialities that are not immediately apparent or commonly understood. Furthermore, contrary to a common misunderstanding both in and outside of Masonry, in philosophy and spirituality, the esoteric is not limited to secret teachings about metaphysics, whether models of divine hierarchies, planes of manifestation, levels of consciousness, practical methods of mystical prayer, or approaches to working with subtle energy. The desire to delve into such matters actually comes from our deeper, more essential, and even instinctive desire to unveil the unknown and grasp the mysteries of existence. *This very rudimentary human desire to make the unknown known is the essential motivation of esotericism.*

While there are important scholarly definitions of esotericism that are relevant to our Craft, for the present purposes, we set them aside in order to make a fresh and more broadly accessible approach to Masonic esotericism. A Masonic form of esotericism would have things in common with the more esoteric domains in other fields of endeavor. For example, quantum physicists qualify as esotercists of physical science because they are concerned with aspects of matter and energy that are not directly observable with the senses alone. Depth psychologists are esotericists of psychology because they seek to understand the inner workings of the human mind that are not immediately observable through physical behavior or ordinary cognition. Mystics are esotericists of spirituality because they dive into the ecstatic and ineffable dimensions of devotion to Deity. Likewise, Masonic esotericists are Masons who seek to understand the inner or hidden aspects of Masonry, which include not only deeper interpretations of its symbolism and ritual, but also the internal psychological challenges of actually following its principles, tenets, and instructions. In other words, in its most basic sense, *Masonic esotericism is the perception that there are mysterious depths within Masonry coupled with the effort to plumb those depths in our own lives.* Contemplative Masonry may thus be more specifically regarded as the actual practice of plumbing those depths through inner work, which we will directly address in the following chapters of this book.

Beginning with this definition, it can easily be shown that an esoteric approach in Masonry is not only possible, but that it is actually intended to be part of the academic, philosophical, and spiritual initiations offered by our tradition. Masonry's own words consistently encourage such perceptions, desires, and efforts through repeated attention to that which is "internal," through the use of the term "speculative" to define our Craft, through symbolism and allegory as teaching methods, and through its encouragement for Masons to be studious, prayerful, contemplative, and virtuous. Furthermore, among our central allegorical allusions are the symbolic quests for light and the Lost Word. To argue that there is nothing inherently esoteric about Masonry would thus require a more narrow definition of "esoteric." It is therefore somewhat redundant to qualify Masonry and Masons with terms like "esoteric Masonry," "Masonic esotericism," "Masonic esotericist," or "contemplative Mason," although they are useful in emphasizing the special attention being given to the internal or hidden aspects of our Craft.

What, then, would characterize a *straightforward* approach to Masonic esotericism? First, by "straightforward," we mean an approach that stems directly from our traditional rituals and teachings and requires neither familiarity with other traditions nor starting with a focus on metaphysics. Of course, we are free to explore such possibilities, and some Masons have personally found it worthwhile to do so, but it is presumptive to say they are necessarily parts of anyone's approach to Masonic esotericism. Second, a straightforward approach would make use of resources and human faculties commonly employed in any esoteric pursuit; no unusual abilities would be needed, although the work might lead one to develop certain faculties in new ways. Whether in the sciences, such as physics or psychology, or in the domain of religion, the esotericists are those who not only study and work with that which is superficially obvious, they also penetrate into that which is hidden by employing abstract reasoning, exercising their imaginations, attending to their intuitions, and opening their hearts and minds to inspiration. It should be clear to every Mason that our ritual teachings actually encourage such an approach to Masonry, and thereby to every aspect of our lives as social, moral, intellectual, and spiritual beings.

It is one thing to grasp the philosophical basis of an esoteric approach to Masonry, but as with other esoteric pursuits, there should also be a practical dimension. In other words, in order to fully engage Masonic esotericism we should include actual practices that are especially fitting in the Masonic milieu. It is therefore interesting, and perhaps frustrating to some of us, that our tradition encourages such things without offering much explicit technical guidance. This fact has undoubtedly contributed to the somewhat popular notion that Masonry is meant to lead to another system of esoteric thought and practice. However, it can be argued that there are elements of our ritual and its teachings that strongly suggest actual practices which require no special knowledge of other traditions or specific systems. The following paragraphs make that argument by highlighting some relevant elements of our tradition and corresponding methods that fit within a straightforward approach to Masonic esotericism.

SPECULATIVE THINKING

Our tradition teaches that we are engaged in *Speculative Masonry* rather than Operative Masonry. While we have ritual instructions on this distinction, it is also worthwhile to simply consider the meaning of "speculative." To be speculative is to ask and try to answer questions such as these:

- What might a particular thing symbolize or mean other than what is superficially or literally apparent?
- If we consider something to have a particular meaning or explanation, how might that affect the possible meanings or explanations of other things?
- Where are the gaps in our explanations, knowledge, and understanding, and what possibilities might fill in the gaps?
- What other explanations are possible for the way things are?

Our tradition illustrates that for centuries, Speculative Masons have applied these kinds of questions to the tools, methods, and customs of stonemasonry. Our ritual clearly engages this process by regarding almost everything we experience or do in the lodge as emblematic, symbolic, or allegorical of something related to virtuous and moral living. Masonic esotericism does not assume that all the speculative thinking in Masonry has already been done for us by the early ritualists, or that our only duties are to learn and perpetuate what they found. In fact, the ritual and monitorial instructions of many jurisdictions encourage us to always seek more light. Masonic esotericism therefore takes the ritual's explanations as a common foundation while also answering its call to attain new insight, understanding, and wisdom. In support of this approach, consider these very explicit statements from the *Monitor of the Lodge* (Grand Lodge of Texas A.F. & A.M., 1982). The emphasis is given as in the original cited text:

> *"Masonry does not expound the truths concealed in her emblems. It displays the symbols and may give a hint here and there concerning some characteristic of its several meanings, but it must remain for the Neophite to search out for himself the more hidden significations."* (p. xvi)

> *"It [the Lodge] is said to be opened **on**, and not **in**, a certain degree (which latter expression is often incorrectly used), in reference rather to the speculative, than to the legal character, of the meeting; to indicate, not that the members are to be circumscribed **in** the limits of a particular degree, but that they are met together to unite in contemplation **on** the*

symbolic teachings and divine lessons, to inculcate which is the peculiar object of that degree." (p. 4)

"*An Illustrious Masonic Scholar [Albert Pike] has well said, 'He who would become an accomplished Mason must not be content merely to hear or even to understand the lectures, but must, aided by them and then having as it were the way marked out for him, study, interpret, and develop these symbols for himself.*'" (p. 23)

To summarize, as individuals and together in our lodges, our tradition urges us to engage in speculative thinking about the symbolism of our tradition. This aspect of esotericism, an entry into at least an academic initiation, is not something grafted onto Masonry by a few members with special interests, but rather, it is an innate aspect of Masonry itself. Speculative thinking is therefore offered in this article as the first and most common support for Masons pursuing the esoteric work of our Craft.

DISCOURSE

In the previous citations from the *Texas Monitor*, it is stated that one of the purposes of opening a lodge is for members to join together in speculative thinking. The significance of sharing our questions and insights with each other is further addressed by the following monitorial instructions for each of the three Craft degrees, respectively:

"*At your leisure hours, that you may improve in Masonic knowledge, you are to converse with well informed brethren, who will always be as ready to give, as you are to receive instruction."* (p. 28)

"The wise and beneficent Author of Nature intended, by the formation of this sense [hearing], that we should be social creatures, and to receive the greatest and most important part of our knowledge by intercourse with each other. For these purposes we are endowed with hearing, that, by a proper exertion of our rational powers, our happiness may be complete." (p. 53)

*"Thus was man formed for social and active life; the noblest part of the work of God; and he that will so demean himself as not to be endeavoring to add to the common stock of knowledge and understanding, may be deemed a **drone** in the **hive** of nature, a useless member of society, and unworthy of our protection as Masons."* (p. 81)

Note the admonition to be active and add to knowledge and understanding. Obviously this calls for more than memorizing and regurgitating the words of those who came before us.

Educated in classical philosophy, learned Masons of the 18th and 19th centuries were well familiar with time-tested methods of discourse, such as lecture and response and the dialectics of various philosophers. Discourse was then, and still is, an indispensible method of refining the skills of logic and rhetoric, which are among the liberal arts earnestly recommended by our ritual to polish and adorn the minds of Masons. By their own experience, our ancient brethren would have known that the various forms of discourse not only provide opportunities to give and receive ideas and information, but also to enjoy these benefits:

- a stronger sense of belonging, companionship, and other conditions of social initiation;
- evaluation of the evidence and logic in each other's thinking;
- exposure of errors and superfluities;
- comparison, contrast, and assimilation with other ideas and information;
- eliciting previously unseen possibilities;
- stimulation for the discovery of new and more meaningful ideas and information.

While the study of classical philosophy can certainly enhance one's potentials with discourse, it is not necessary. Discourse is a common element of our contemporary educational methods and social lives; we first learn to use it without even being aware that we are doing so. In the ordinary functions of any Masonic lodge, the exchange of questions and answers among officers actually models the practice of discourse, as does the exchange of questions and answers by which Masons are tested for proficiency in a degree. Yet, if we only parrot the words we have inherited, failing to learn and apply the actual processes these exchanges illustrate, then we are merely performing rote recitation, not discourse, and thus shortchanging our experience and practice of Masonry. The traditional forms in lodge constantly provide occasions for members to ask speculative questions or to share ideas and information about their understanding and application of Masonry's symbols and allegories. Many lodges set aside time in their regular meetings or call special meetings specifically for such purposes. Furthermore, prior to the closing of every duly opened lodge, the Worshipful Master always asks if anyone has anything to offer for the good of the Craft. So it is that in both word and deed Masonry encourages us to join in discourse as an element of Masonic esotericism.

STUDY

Study is actually one of the most overtly and specifically touted activities in our tradition, and certainly most easily identifiable as an aspect of an academic, and perhaps philosophical, initiation. Our ritual and monitorial instructions encourage learning in general, while specifically recommending study of the teachings and symbols of the Craft, of the Great Light in Masonry, of nature, and of various arts and sciences. Masonic esotericists have often pursued studies not only in these traditionally suggested areas, but also in others such as philosophy, psychology, religion, and history, each of which has its own broad range of specialties. Such studies are very appropriate, and it is in this context that some Masonic esotericists find great value in studying other esoteric traditions and delving into metaphysics.

By becoming more informed through their studies, Masons can enhance their practice of speculative thinking and better prepare themselves for discourse. As we engage in study, we have opportunities to not only take in information, but to think about that information critically and speculatively. To study in that way is to enter into a type of internal discourse with the thoughts of the author or authors of the material. In following our particular interests more deeply, more esoterically, we become increasingly knowledgeable in the subtleties, complexities, and diversities of a particular field as well as its interconnectedness with others. Thus many of the benefits previously noted for the practice of discourse can come to us through the performance of research and reflection in our studies.

MEDITATION

> *"**Initiation** is to be attained only after real labor, deep study, profound meditation, extensive research and a constant practice of those virtues which will open a true path to moral, intellectual and spiritual illumination."* (p. xv)

This quote has been borrowed from Albert Pike by the *Texas Monitor*, and it captures much of what we have already considered while also highlighting "profound meditation" as a key part of Masonic esotericism. The glossary of the *Texas Monitor* then draws attention to the connection between meditation and contemplation in the entries for "Contemplative" and "Meditating." Both of these entries allude to the practice of thoughtful, deliberative consideration, revealing that the terms are commonly interchangeable. It is therefore reasonable to consider how our ritual and monitorial instructions encourage us to practice meditation when they speak of contemplation.

"It is, of course, impracticable, and inexpedient, in a monitorial work, to give a full explanation of the various symbols and ceremonies of our important rites; but an allusion … will be sufficient to lead the observant and contemplative Mason to make further examination into their more concealed and important import." (p. 12)

"On this theme [of Truth] we contemplate…." (p. 34)

*"The second section * * * * and treats of Masonry under two denominations, Operative and Speculative. It also details some interesting features relative to the Temple of Solomon, and the usages of our Ancient Brethren, in the course of which the mind is drawn to the contemplation of themes of science and philosophy."* (p. 44)

"It [Speculative Masonry] leads the contemplative to view, with reverence and admiration, the glorious works of creation, and inspires him with the most exalted ideas of the perfection of his Divine Creator." (p. 45)

"Contemplating these bodies [the two globes], we are inspired with due reverence for the Deity and his works, and are induced to encourage the studies of Geometry, Astronomy, Geography, and Navigation, and the arts and sciences dependent upon them…." (p. 48)

"They [the ninth or last class of emblems on the Master's Carpet] afford subjects of serious and solemn reflection to the rational and contemplative mind…." (p. 86)

These passages allude to the significant role meditation plays in philosophical and spiritual initiations. Sharing similar recognitions, many philosophical and spiritual traditions offer formal methods of meditative practice, yet Masonry provides no explicit instructions on its actual performance. Here is where we should look more carefully at what our tradition has us do in the course of ritual, rather than reflect only upon its words and images, for the actions of ritual are often as symbolic as the words and images. It is therefore suggested that divestiture and hoodwinking, our earliest ritual experiences, are relevant to the practice of meditation. When our degree candidates are being prepared for entry into the lodge, they must strip away all things that identify them with the profane world and be deprived of the sight of external things. In *Duncan's Ritual and Monitor* (3rd ed., Malcom C. Duncan, 1976) one of the most popular and accurate exposures of contemporary Masonic ritual, this moment of hood-winking is footnoted with a reference to the entry on "Darkness" in Albert Mackey's *Lexicon of Freemasonry*, which says:

> *"DARKNESS among Freemasons is emblematical of ignorance; for as our science has technically been called 'LUX,' or light, the absence of light must be the absence of knowledge. Hence the rule that the **eye should not see until the heart has conceived** the true nature of those beauties which constitute the mysteries of our Order. Freemasonry has restored Darkness to its proper place, as a state of preparation."* (p. 48)

The candidate is thus allegorically stripped of both the material and intellectual possessions by which all humans tend to identify themselves and is thereby left in a state of preparation for something more meaningful. Ask people who they are, and they may tell of their occupations, the things they own, who they know and love, or perhaps describe their beliefs and values. Then ask them to strip away those things and speak to who they are, and most will pause to turn silently inward in search of something more meaningful, more profound, more mysterious, or more esoteric. They may or may not realize it, but in that moment, their silence is an admission of ignorance about the deeper and more essential aspects of being, an ignorance that even the most illuminated sages have confessed always remains with them to some degree. Our ritual and monitorial instructions draw attention to these deeper aspects of our being in countless ways, including these more obvious statements:

> *"It has also been said that the word 'Masonry,' in addition to the significations already named, and others which cannot be properly specified here, signifies a vast and comprehensive body of **knowledge**, **teachings**, **traditions**, and **principles**, concerning the visible universe ... as well as the operations and sublime moral principles and processes of the human mind."* (Texas Monitor, p. xii)

> *"On the mind all our knowledge must depend; what, therefore, can be a more proper subject for the investigation of Masons? To sum up the whole of this transcendent measure of God's bounty to man, we shall add that memory, imagination, reasoning, moral perception, and all the active powers of the soul, including its senses, present a vast and boundless field for study and investigation, and are peculiar mysteries, known only to nature and nature's God, to Whom we are all indebted for creation, preservation, and every blessing we enjoy."* (p. 55)

Returning to reflection upon the actual events of our rituals, we know that candidates prepared to enter the lodge are both destitute and in a state of darkness. In many lodges, it is customary for them to then sit alone, silently, for some period of time before they are guided in their next steps. In addition to the previously stated allegorical explanations, it should be noted that this condition parallels the most basic and universal technique of formal meditation, which is simply to close one's eyes and be still and silent. Silent sitting meditation is therefore offered as a most fitting practice for Masonic inner work, and even an indispensable practice for anyone wanting to receive all the light their Masonic experience can bestow.

The benefits of silent sitting are significant, and in them we find many reasons that this simple form of meditation has been practiced in many cultures and all ages, and why it should be recommended to any Mason, more especially those desiring philosophical or spiritual initiation. When the eyes are closed and attention is turned inward, a relaxation of the body and calming of the mind naturally begins. Many traditions teach that focusing upon the flow of the breath further enhances the shift to a more peaceful and centered state of consciousness. Respiration becomes more efficient, the pulse and blood pressure typically lower, and the mind grows quieter. This state may itself be the primary aim of a person's practice, and there is a growing body of research that provides evidence of its benefits to physical, psychological, and social wellbeing, including an improved ability to focus attention. In that regard, silent sitting is often practiced as "state of preparation" for meditation upon something in particular, such as a word, image, or event, with the intention of gaining deeper insight and understanding about it. Thus silent sitting is also excellent preparation for other aspects of Masonic esotericism. Privately, it can serve as a transition into study or the opening of an internal lodge for our moments of solitary speculation. When done together with other Masons, it can help establish both an internal and external atmosphere that is more conducive to discourse and the contemplative performance of ritual.

Before leaving this consideration of silent sitting, we should consider a very typical experience that arises in its practice. When eyes are closed, perceptions of the external world are gradually released, and attention is turned inward. In this state, the mind has nothing to observe other than its own content and processes: "memory, imagination, reasoning, moral perception, and all the active powers of the soul, including its senses." In these moments of profound self-awareness, we are directly grasping the quintessential working tool of Masonry, which is consciousness itself. If Masonry concerns itself first with the internal qualities of its members, then surely there is no internal Masonic labor more appropriate than this. We find that it does indeed "present a vast and boundless field for study and investigation." As people begin meditating upon their own consciousness, it is quite normal for them to realize how little they have understood and mastered this tool that enables them to use all other tools. A common part of this process is the frustration that can arise when one tries to make the mind become more still and quiet. The very effort of doing so can actually stir mental activity, and thereby set in motion a self-defeating feedback loop. While some people mistakenly conclude that this means they don't have the ability to meditate, others take it as one among many clues that the soul is filled with "peculiar mysteries" that they have just entered as apprentices.

Finally, no discussion of meditation and contemplation would be complete without addressing prayer, which is certainly a ubiquitous element of Masonic work. Masonry teaches us that all important undertakings should start with an invocation of Deity and that all our work should be performed in honor of the Great Architect of the Universe. Our traditional prayers for lodge meetings and ceremonies serve not only these purposes, but are also short meditations intended to draw our attention to particular attitudes, principles, and aims that are conducive to our Masonic labors. We can also benefit from prayer performed in these ways at the beginning and ending of all our moments of private study and meditation. Furthermore, because personal, private prayer often starts by turning attention inward and then becomes a spontaneous outpouring of one's fears, desires, hopes, and thanks, it can be a form of meditation that offers an excellent opportunity to observe and evaluate the content and workings of one's own soul. Additionally, the prayer of silence, of simply being attentive and receptive to the presence of the Divine, is highly esteemed in a variety of contemplative traditions, where it is regarded as the unveiling of the Sanctum Sanctorum within the temple (con-*templum*) of one's own consciousness. In summary, any Mason who earnestly engages in prayer is doing a key part of the inner, or esoteric, work in our tradition.

VIRTUE

At the beginning of the previous section, the monitorial quote highlighted the importance of virtue as a Masonic practice. In fact, nearly everything previously cited makes it clear that our pursuit of light is intended to improve us in virtue. Furthermore, every working tool, jewel, emblem, furnishing of the lodge, and legend is useful to us in terms of developing virtuous thought and action. Our tradition teaches that through an active commitment to understanding and living these lessons, we make ourselves of greater benefit to ourselves, our fellow human beings, and, as may be one's religious faith and hope, thereby become more pleasing to the Great Architect of the Universe. Of all the proposed elements of Masonic esotericism, none is more obviously spelled out for us than the practice of virtue. Even so, a mere cursory reading or recitation of our lessons can easily fail to grasp their profundity and the implications for how to actually apply them. The work of virtue, as external or exoteric as it may seem, has significant esoteric depths. As we move into them, we should not merely put on the moral and social virtues of Masonry like a façade on a weak and empty structure. Rather, we should strive to properly develop our virtues from the inside out, just as the proper construction of a house develops from foundation to frame, then to walls and roof, and finally to its furniture and decorations.

One of our most basic and broadly applicable lessons on the development of virtue as inner work is found in the Entered Apprentice degree's instructions on the gavel and the ashlar. It expressly draws an analogy between the ashlar and "the mind and conscience" of the individual Mason; the ashlar is thus an emblem of the soul. The word "conscience" also reminds us that there is a reciprocal relationship between the internal operations of the soul and our external behavior in this world, and thus provides a key to how one performs the work of the gavel. The gavel serves as an emblem of the force of will, intelligently and carefully guided to chip away thoughts and behaviors that might distract us from being more virtuous. The operation of the gavel is therefore not just an external modification of behavior, but involves one's whole being. Anyone who has sincerely attempted to rectify the thought patterns and behaviors of a deeply ingrained vice knows how much this work is internal in nature. Aside from the difficulty in overcoming the sheer momentum of habitual thoughts and actions, most vices have emotional payoffs that we continue to desire and that tempt us to relapse. Additionally, we can be so crafty at creating excuses and justifications for our vices that we can even fool ourselves into regarding them as necessities, if not masking them as virtues. So it is that while the work of the gavel may seem to be more letting go of vice than building of virtue, in order for it to be effective, one must exercise the virtue of self-awareness.

The inner work of building virtue benefits greatly from the practice of mindfulness, which is being as present, attentive, and careful as possible in both the internal and external dimensions of one's experiences *as they are happening*. Likewise, reflection upon our actions, or meditatively studying them in hindsight, is also revealed as highly valuable, especially introspective reflections in which we evaluate our own thoughts, feelings, and actions. These practices of mindfulness and reflection are alluded to by the many testing and measuring devices we symbolically employ; the rule, plumb, level, and square are instruments that must constantly be applied in the proper construction and inspection of any edifice. Mindfulness and reflection are therefore the keys to the fundamental virtue of self-awareness, and are thus complimentary to the practice of meditation. Without them, the raw force of will, even with the best of intentions, can too easily be wasted or do actual harm rather than good. An excellent starting place for the application of the force of will is thus in the commitment to continually and more thoroughly integrate the practices of mindfulness and reflection in all aspects of our lives.

With all the virtues taught by Masonry, it is reasonable to ask if there is some particular virtue that reigns supreme, one that can serve as a constant guide and test for all that we think and do. Self-awareness may be the foundational virtue for the development of others, but what virtue most inspires the heart to conceive of the beauties possible for one's conduct and relationships? While each of us is free to reach his own conclusions in this matter, for now, it is suggested that we consider love as the answer Masonry most often provides to such questions. Love is so central to our tradition that we repeatedly find it touched upon throughout our degrees.

We begin our consideration of love as the guiding virtue with the most obvious references to it in the Entered Apprentice degree: the principle tenets, the northeast corner, and the third of the theological virtues. Among the principle tenets, brotherly love obviously relates to the present theme, yet we can further discern that relief does as well. What is relief if not the caring and compassionate effort to reduce or eliminate the burden of another? Relief of a "distressed worthy brother" is so revered that on the 24-inch gauge it is even accorded to the same section as the service of God! Likewise, the traditional explanation of truth is not merely an intellectual abstraction about discernment and honesty; instead, it is an exhortation to replace hypocrisy and deceit with sincerity and forthrightness in both our hearts and our words, and thereby promote and rejoice in each other's wellbeing. Charity, which is the lesson of the northeast corner and the third rung of the theological ladder, clearly connects with love. Indeed, the Latin source of this word, *caritas*, specifically refers to selfless, unconditional, and generous love, or universal benevolence.

As Master Masons, we learn that our special working tool is the trowel, an instrument actually used to spread cement or mortar, but which Speculative Masons use "for the more noble and glorious purpose of spreading the cement of brotherly love and affection." While we are taught this cement should unite us as a harmonious and productive fraternity, it is important to understand that our fraternal relationships are not the only place for the trowel. Masonry often encourages us to extend its lessons into every facet of our lives. For example, consider the third degree's lesson on the bee hive:

> *"...as we came into the world endowed as rational and intelligent beings, so we should ever be industrious ones; never sitting down contented while our fellow creatures around us are in want, when it is in our power to relieve them...."* (p. 81)

In keeping with Masonry's commitment to the betterment of human society at large, we should strive to wield the trowel everywhere, at all times, with all people. In effect, the lesson of the trowel brings us full-circle to rediscover the very thing that made it possible for us to enter the lodge as candidates. We asked, sought, and knocked, and we were answered with love.

Midway through our journey in the Craft degrees, we find the following declaration:

> *"Geometry, or Masonry (originally synonymous terms), being of divine and moral nature, is enriched with the most useful knowledge; while it proves the wonderful properties of nature, it demonstrates the more important truths of morality."* (p. 63)

Relationship is the common principle that makes the analogy between (1) the properties of nature and (2) the truths of morality; the first concerns the physical relationships between the various dimensions of objects in space, and the second concerns the social and spiritual relationships between human souls. Masonry teaches us that the geometry of human relationships should be moral, by which we understand that it should be characterized by virtues such as equity, benevolence, and conscientiousness, or, in a word, love. Thus we can discern that Masonry itself is the craft of being and becoming ever more loving to all our fellow human beings. Every part of our ritual and symbolism is intended to guide and support us in developing the more specific virtues, each of which constitutes some particular way of thinking and acting in service of love. It is therefore most fitting for us to keep love as the constant reference point of our mindfulness and reflections in the practice of virtue.

SUMMARY

In reviewing the main points of this chapter, it might occur to the reader that a straightforward summary of this "straightforward" approach to Masonic esotericism amounts to this – take all that Masonry offers and do these things with it:

- speculate about it;
- talk with other Masons about it;
- carefully study it and relevant subjects that interest you;
- meditate upon it;
- and practice its virtues mindfully, reflectively, and, most of all, lovingly.

To complete this summary, it should be noted that while the practice of each point has its own value, each also supports and enhances the others. They are therefore not steps in a sequential process, but together, form a more comprehensive way of diving into explorations and applications of Masonry in our lives. In this way, Masonic esotericism is immediately accessible to every Mason and is not merely the specialty of members interested in metaphysics or the esotericism of other philosophical and spiritual traditions. In fact, esotericism already is, and seems to have always been, an indispensable part of living our tradition to the fullest. The next three chapters will provide a comprehensive set of practical exercises for actually doing the inner work of Masonic esotericism.

"All through the Masonic Tradition, the neophyte is taught that he is to be engaged thenceforth in the preparation of material and the actual building of a spiritual Temple, an house not made with hands, eternal in the heavens.... Now the peculiarity of the Masonic building operation is this; that the Masonic brother is at one and the same time _both builder and building material_."

George W. Plummer,
"Living Stones," Esoteric Masonry

THE INNER WORK OF AN ENTERED APPRENTICE

"A dim consciousness of infinite mystery and grandeur lies beneath the commonplace of life. So we live our little life; but Heaven is above us and all around and close to us; and Eternity is before us and behind us; and suns and stars are silent witnesses and watchers over us. We are enfolded by Infinity." — Albert Pike, Morals and Dogma

MINDFUL AND PRAYERFUL BEHAVIOR

As you begin your work in contemplative Masonry, here is a very simple point recommended as a cornerstone tenet: contemplative Masonry is not just an academic approach to Masonry - it is a *lifestyle*. That assertion does not mean that you have to start living your life completely differently. The contemplative lifestyle seeks to plumb the depths and clearly grasp the reality of any given situation, to be fully present in the here-and-now moment of authentic experience. The experiences you choose for your life are up to you. You may begin to adopt the contemplative lifestyle simply by practicing mindful and prayerful behavior throughout your waking hours. Such work is especially recommended when you are involved in Masonic activities.

Mindful behavior is a state of conscious action in which we attend with all of our faculties to whatever it is we are actually doing. The challenge of mindful behavior is to live each moment with conscious intent, reducing the degree to which we behave in habitual, automatic, and unconscious ways. In our modern world, it is common for an individual to be doing some routine task such as driving to work while simultaneously trying to listen to the news on the radio, thinking about what must be done upon arrival at work, and feeling left-over emotions from a marital spat of the previous night. All too often we try to juggle any number of activities, feelings, and concerns, not realizing that in so doing we cannot possibly give any one of them a truly adequate degree of attention. As a result, we make mistakes, become confused, fail to learn, forget things, misjudge situations, misinterpret the actions and words of others, and get caught in accidents. In many cases, such chaotic behavior leads to serious relationship problems, stress reactions, physical and mental illness, and even death.

The only solution to this pattern is to focus as much as possible on one thing at a time. Mindful behavior places our focus on the task at hand, no matter how simple or routine it may be. In fact, it is an effective way of becoming grounded and gaining composure in the midst of turmoil. In order to practice mindful behavior, begin paying attention to your senses in this very moment. Notice the colors, shapes, textures, temperatures, movements, sounds, smells, and tastes that are involved in the immediate situation. Rather than analyzing or evaluating them, simply be as aware of them as possible. In addition to your senses, notice how you are responding emotionally. What are you feeling in your gut and in your heart? Direct your thinking to focus on the situation. Are you acting with conscious intent or automatically? Are you becoming distracted by stray thoughts?

If you begin to practice mindful behavior on a regular basis, you may at first feel that it is slowing you down, that you won't have time to think about and do all the things that you want to do. In many cases, this may be nothing more than an irrational sense of anxiety brought about by the change of your focus. We all get used to doing things in certain ways, and when we begin to change, it can feel awkward and uncomfortable. However, such feelings may also reveal that you have not been adequately organizing your life, that your priorities are not clear, or that you have allowed your life to become unwisely complicated. In these cases, mindful behavior actually helps us see where and how to bring greater order and harmony to our lives.

Beyond immediate awareness of your sensations, emotions, and thoughts, there is still another level of mindful behavior, and that is *prayerful* behavior. In this context, we are not talking about *saying* prayers so much as practicing a reverent attitude. Prayerful behavior remains open to the Divine Presence in every moment. It seeks to maintain communication with your own spirit and the intuition, creativity, and wisdom that can flow from it. In prayerful behavior, every act may be expressed as an act of love, devotion, and honor to God, another person, yourself, or all of these together. This kind of action and attitude has the potential to raise your consciousness beyond a personal perspective, illuminating the moment as the eternal ongoing manifestation of the Divine Will.

Mindful and prayerful behavior does not mean that we never take the time to reflect upon the past, plan for the future, or muse about possibilities. It means that when it is time to do these things, we do them with clear intent and focus. As you progress through the exercises of this book, you will learn more about the tools and methods that you can use to maximize the benefits of such times.

MINDFUL AND PRAYERFUL BEHAVIOR IN MASONIC ACTIVITIES

As a contemplative Mason, it is especially important that you practice mindful and prayerful behavior in Masonic activities. Under this heading we include degree rituals, lodge meetings, and various Masonic functions. In addition, we also give special attention to our interactions with other Masons in any place at any time, as well as speaking, reading or writing about Masonry. In some cases, practitioners may not have access to Masonic activities more than once per month. In order to facilitate progress in such cases, it is recommended that the following exercises be applied to some other regular activity, such as attendance of religious services. One can then return to these exercises to complete them within a Masonic atmosphere.

(Note: To get the most benefit from these and future exercises, you will need a journal in which to record what you have done and experienced. There is a great deal of benefit in keeping a journal, and for that reason you will be consistently reminded to make notes in yours.)

EXERCISE 1:1

At the next Masonic function you attend, make every effort to closely attend to your physical sensations as you experience the event. Even aspects that we normally take for granted, such as the opening and closing of the lodge, should be carefully observed. You will naturally experience emotions and thoughts as well, but keep directing your awareness to the actual physical experience that you perceive by sight, sound, touch, taste, and smell. To help you maintain focus, do not arrive early and do not stay late. Avoid superfluous and idle talk, but be courteous and considerate, as every Mason should on all occasions. As soon as you arrive home, take some time to recall and reflect upon your sensations. Make note of anything new or unusual about the physical sensations you experienced during the event. Record your answers to the following questions:

- How would you list your senses in order of the amount of information you received?
- How did the focus on your sensations add to or subtract from the way the event affected you?
- If the event was something you have witnessed or participated in before, what sensations did you notice that you tend to tune out of your experience?
- If you were to do this exercise again, what would you do differently?

EXERCISE 1:2

After having completed Exercise 1:1, at the next Masonic function that you attend, make every effort to closely attend to your emotions as you experience the event. You will naturally experience sensations and thoughts as well, but keep directing your awareness to the emotions that you experience in your gut and heart. To help you maintain focus, do not arrive early and do not stay late. Avoid superfluous and idle talk. As soon as you arrive home, take some time to recall and reflect upon your emotions. Make note of anything new or unusual about the feelings you experienced in your gut and heart. Record your answers to the following questions:

- How would you list your emotions in order of the strength and frequency that you experienced them?
- How did the focus on your emotions add to or subtract from the way the event affected you?

- If the event was something you have witnessed or participated in before, what emotions did you notice that you tend to tune out of your experience?
- If you were to do this exercise again, what would you do differently?

EXERCISE 1:3

After having completed Exercise 1:2, at the next Masonic function that you attend, make every effort to closely attend to your mental activity as you experience the event. You will naturally experience sensations and emotions as well, but keep directing your awareness to the thoughts and images that you experience in your mind. To help you maintain focus, do not arrive early and do not stay late. Avoid superfluous and idle talk. As soon as you arrive home, take some time to recall and reflect upon your thoughts. Make note of anything new or unusual about the thoughts and images you experienced. Record your answers to the following questions:

- How would you list your thoughts and images in order of the significance and meaning that you experienced in them?
- How did the focus on your thoughts and imagination add to or subtract from the way the event affected you?

- If the event was something you have witnessed or participated in before, what thoughts and images did you notice that you tend to tune out of your experience?

- If you were to do this exercise again, what would you do differently?

EXERCISE 1:4

After having completed Exercise 1:3, at the next Masonic function that you attend, make every effort to closely attend to your spirit as you experience the event. You will naturally experience sensations, emotions, and thoughts as well, but keep directing your awareness to remain open to the mysteries of your spirit and the presence of the Divine. To help you maintain focus, do not arrive early and do not stay late. Avoid superfluous and idle talk. As soon as you arrive home, take some time to recall and reflect upon your experience. Make note of anything new or unusual about the experience. Record your answers to the following questions:

- How would you describe your experience in terms of intuition, inspiration, creativity, will, or awareness of your spirit and the Divine?

- How did the focus on your spirit add to or subtract from the way the event affected you?

- If the event was something you have witnessed or participated in before, what did you notice that you tend to tune out of your experience?
- If you were to do this exercise again, what would you do differently?

EXERCISE 1:5

After having completed Exercise 1:4, at the next Masonic function that you attend, make every effort to closely attend to your total experience of the event, being mindful of all levels of your being. You will naturally experience imbalances and distractions, but keep directing your awareness to each level. To help you maintain focus, do not arrive early and do not stay late. Avoid superfluous and idle talk. As soon as you arrive home, take some time to recall and reflect upon your experience. Make note of anything new or unusual about the experience. Record your answers to the following questions:

- How would you list the different levels in order of the meaning you found in them?
- How did the simultaneous focus on all levels add to or subtract from the way the event affected you?
- If the event was something you have witnessed or participated in before, what did you notice that you tend to tune out of your experience?
- If you were to do this exercise again, what would you do differently?

You are advised to repeat Exercise 1:5 a few more times before moving on to the next exercise. Furthermore, you are advised to continue practicing mindful and prayerful behavior at all times, but especially when engaged in Masonic activities.

"If the reader will but reflect a moment on his own process of breathing, he will find that the inbreathing (inhalation) and the outbreathing (exhalation) are equal, and equally active processes, although so different, each being the opposite of the other: each, in its turn, the cause of the other. Stop one, and the other ceases also. The more one reflects on this symbol of the Great Breath which creation is, the more will he understand of both Eternal Nature and his own being."
— J.D. Buck, *Mystic Masonry*

BREATH

It can be argued that the fundamental element of life is breath. We may go many days without food and a few without water, but our physical lives will end after only a few minutes without air. In many languages, the words that express the essence or higher levels of our being are closely related to the words for breath, wind, or air. As an example, consider the similarities between the English words **spirit**, **inspiration**, and **respirator**. The etymology of these words leads back to the Latin **spiritus**, which literally means "breath." In Hebrew, the three most commonly used words for soul – *nephesh*, *ruach*, and *neschamah* – are also used for breath. In fact, the book of Genesis literally says that God breathed life into Adam. The Chinese word *chi* also refers to the breath of life. There are other examples, but the basic point is that our most ancient languages and texts reflect awareness that breath is central to life. As a contemplative Mason, you will pay closer attention to your breath, and you will learn to use it to affect your awareness, mood, and behavior.

EXERCISE 1:6

For one week, set aside a few minutes once or twice a day to be mindful and prayerful in your breathing. Do not attempt to interfere with it or regulate it in any way. Simply pay attention to the way that you breathe and how it changes in different situations from the moment you awaken in the morning until the moment you fall asleep at night. Make daily notes in your journal, including answers to the following questions:

- How much of your day do you naturally tend to breathe slowly and easily, with a relaxed belly, chest, and throat?

- Considering these three body regions, how would you rank them in order of how much you tend to keep them tensed or tightened?
- How do different physical activities affect the rate, depth, and regions of your breathing?
- How do different emotional states affect your breathing?
- How does simply becoming mindful of your breathing affect it?
- What occurred to you as you were prayerful in your breathing?

EXERCISE 1:7

For one week, set aside a few minutes once or twice a day to practice relaxed, natural breathing. Sit in a chair with your feet on the floor, your back supported and erect, and your neck straight. Close your eyes and focus on the sensations of your breathing. Relax your throat, chest, and belly. Feel the way the air flows in through your nostrils or lips, down your throat, and into your lungs. Notice that when you are relaxed, you pull the breath down with your belly, and that your chest actually does very little work. Feel how your diaphragm naturally forces the air out. Feel it flowing out of your lungs, up through your throat, and out your nostrils or lips. It is important to begin breathing through the nose as much as possible. Notice how your body relaxes, your mood calms and your thinking becomes clearer as you focus on your breath. In fact, you may practice this exercise if you find yourself feeling tense or stressed and you wish to relax. After a while you may open your eyes. Make appropriate notes in your journal.

EXERCISE 1:8

For one week, set aside a few minutes once or twice a day to practice deep, cleansing breaths. It is especially recommended that you do so soon after awakening, and you may wish to make it a permanent part of your morning routine. It is also very helpful if you are wearing comfortable, non-restrictive clothing. Sit in a chair with your feet on the floor, your back supported and erect, and your neck straight. Close your eyes and focus on the sensations of your breathing. Relax your throat, chest, and belly. Allow yourself to breathe naturally through your nose for several breaths. At some point, inhale a deep, full breath through your nose, and then hold that breath for a steady count of ten. As you hold the breath, be sure to keep your throat and sinuses open. Use your diaphragm and chest muscles to keep the air in your lungs. Then exhale a full breath through your mouth. It will be necessary to tighten the muscles in your belly and chest a little, but do not strain. Hold the pause between breaths for a steady count of seven. Then, completely relax your belly and chest as you begin another deep inhalation through your nose.

Complete this process through three complete cycles. After the third exhalation and pause, simply relax and return to natural breathing through your nose. Notice how the dramatic increase of oxygen in your blood has affected your body, mind, and emotions. After several natural breaths, you may open your eyes. Make appropriate notes in your journal. Regular use of this technique may help your respiratory and cardiovascular systems. If you already have chronic problems in either of these systems, you should consider consulting a doctor before practicing this exercise.

EXERCISE 1:9

For one week, set aside a few minutes once or twice a day to practice deeply relaxed breathing. It is especially recommended that you do so just before you actually get in bed, and you may wish to make it a permanent part of your evening routine. Sit in a chair with your feet on the floor, your back supported and erect, and your neck straight. Close your eyes and focus on the sensations of your breathing. Relax your throat, chest, and belly. Focus on your breath flowing naturally in and out through your nose. As you continue to breathe naturally and peacefully, begin to count your breaths by mentally saying, "In one, out one. In two, out two." Continue through seven complete cycles of inhale and exhale. If you lose count, start over at one. With each exhale you feel your body becoming more and more relaxed, and your mind becoming more and more quiet and still. You sink deeper and deeper toward a sleep-like state. After the seventh exhale, you may open your eyes. Make appropriate notes in your journal. Regular use of this technique may improve your sleep.

EXERCISE 1:10

For one week, set aside a few minutes once or twice a day to practice rhythmic breathing. Sit in a chair with your feet on the floor, your back supported and erect, and your neck straight. Close your eyes and focus on the sensations of your breathing. Relax your throat, chest, and belly. Focus on your breath flowing naturally in and out through your nose. Use your fingers to feel for your pulse, either in your wrist or in your neck. In your mind, silently keep time with your pulse by repeatedly counting to four. After you have the tempo in your mind, put your hands back in their original positions. Now begin to inhale for a count of four, pause for two, exhale for four and pause for two. Remember that these breaths are supposed to be easy and peaceful. If it seems easier for you to use a six-three or eight-four rhythm, then feel free to make that adjustment. Maintain whatever rhythm you choose and repeat the process through seven complete cycles. After the seventh cycle, you may open your eyes. Make appropriate notes in your journal. Regular use of this technique may help harmonize your mind and body.

"Not only is there a great deal more to light than anyone has ever seen but there are also unknown forms of light which no optical equipment will ever register. There are unnumbered colors which cannot be seen, as well as sounds which cannot be heard, odors which cannot be smelt, flavors which cannot be tasted, and substances which cannot be felt."
— *Manly P. Hall, The Secret Teachings of All Ages*

LET THERE BE LIGHT!

The imagination is an immensely powerful tool. All of us recall the power of our imaginations when we were children. As adults, some of us are quite capable of visualizing and manipulating things in our minds. We may have even brought with us the ability to daydream with such intensity that we temporarily forget our physical surroundings. Through the use of imagery, we can enter a world in which there are no distractions from experiencing and examining whatever subject we choose. The spiritual exercises of St. Ignatius of Loyola, the pathworking of modern Hermeticism, and the visualizations of Qi Gong are examples of the use of imagination for contemplative purposes. In the following exercises, you will sharpen your ability to use your imagination as a tool for contemplation.

You have senses in your imagination, just as you do in your physical body. In order for the imagination to be as useful as possible, you must learn to experience those senses with greater clarity and direct them with greater discipline. The following exercises will guide you through that process for the most useful tools of the imagination, hearing, seeing, and feeling. As a Mason, you know that the senses are addressed in the Fellow Craft degree, and you will contemplate that fact in a later exercise. For now, simply focus on the exercises given in this section.

EXERCISE 1:11

Set aside a few minutes once or twice a day for at least a week to practice this exercise. Complete Exercise 1:10 of the *Breath* section, except that you will not open your eyes after the seventh cycle of rhythmic breathing. Instead, speak aloud a word or short phrase; your name might be a good choice. Repeat that word or phrase several times, listening carefully to the details of the sounds coming from your mouth. Resist any temptation to visualize imagery related to the word or phrase by refocusing on the details of the sounds. At some point, stop speaking aloud. Rather, as you exhale, speak clearly in your mind, reproducing the same details of the sounds. You may wish to alternate speaking aloud and speaking mentally. On another occasion, you might choose to make some sound such as the ring of a bell or a note from a musical instrument. Whatever you choose, you should use only that sound for that session. End each session when you reach a point where no further improvement seems likely. Make appropriate notes in your journal.

EXERCISE 1:12

The title of this section, *Let there be Light!*, alludes to the central importance of the sight aspect of the imagination. Take a moment to consider this point: Being able to see in your imagination must mean that there is some energy within your mind that is analogous to the light by which you see in the material world.

Set aside a few minutes once or twice a day for at least a week to practice this exercise. Begin by choosing some small inanimate object and place it on a table or desk in front of you. You may use any simple three-dimensional object, such as a piece of fruit, a coin, a book, or a lamp. Complete Exercise 1:10 of the *Breath* section. When you open your eyes after the seventh cycle of breath, gaze intently at the object you have chosen. Notice all of its details without touching it. At some point, coordinate an inhalation with the slow closing of your eyes, drawing the image of the object into your mind. Breathe naturally as you examine the image in your mind, seeing the same details that you saw with your physical eyes. At some point, you may open your eyes and repeat the process. Once you have that perspective of the object clearly in your mind, you may move the object so that you see it at another angle. Again, repeat the process of examining the physical details, and then drawing them into your mind. Eventually, you should be able to rotate the image around in your mind, noticing all of the details in a perfect three-dimensional image. End each session when you reach a point where no further improvement seems likely. Make appropriate notes in your journal.

EXERCISE 1:13

You are now going to work with the sense of touch. There are many variables to this sense, but you will focus on texture, pressure, and temperature. Set aside a few minutes once or twice a day for at least a week to practice this exercise. Begin by choosing some small inanimate object and place it on a table or desk in front of you. You may use any simple three-dimensional object. Complete Exercise 1:10 of the *Breath* section. When you open your eyes after the seventh cycle of breath, pick up the object you have chosen. Close your eyes and attend to its texture, the pressure it puts on your skin by its weight, and its temperature. Move it around in your hands and fingers, feeling every part of the object. At some point, put the object down and, with your eyes closed, recall the details of how it felt. In your imagination, feel the same details that you felt with your physical touch. You may repeat the process as often as you like. Resist any tendency to see the object in your imagination by focusing on the feelings. End each session when you reach a point where no further improvement seems likely. Make appropriate notes in your journal.

Exercise *1:14*

Set aside a few minutes once or twice a day for at least a week to practice this exercise. Begin by choosing some visible method of making a sound, such as a clap of your hands, the ring of a bell, the strike of a match, or the rap of a gavel. Complete Exercise 1:10 of the *Breath* section. When you open your eyes after the seventh cycle of breath, make the sound while watching and feeling the action that produces it. Repeat this action several times, paying close attention to every detail of the sound, sight, and feelings of the action. At some point, coordinate the action with an inhalation. Then close your eyes and draw the sound, sight, and feelings of the action into your mind. Now begin to reproduce the details of the sound, sight, and feelings in your mind. You may wish to alternate doing the action physically and mentally. Eventually, you should be able to imagine a perfectly coordinated image of the action, the sound it produces, and the associated feelings. End each session when you reach a point where no further improvement seems likely. Make appropriate notes in your journal.

"We must thoroughly cleanse and purify our hearts to their inmost recesses, before we can of right contemplate that Flaming Star, which is the emblem of the Divine and Glorious Shekinah, or presence of God; before we dare approach the Throne of Supreme Wisdom." — Albert Pike, Morals and Dogma

CENTERING AND CONTEMPLATION

All of the great spiritual traditions of humanity use exercises for centering and focusing consciousness. It is common for these traditions to use techniques involving the visualization and circulation of light. The following exercise has points in common with all of them and provides a simple yet effective means of preparing you to contemplate the symbols, rituals, and tenets of Masonry at deeper levels. From this time forward, the centering exercise will be the foundation of your contemplative work.

EXERCISE 1:15 - THE CENTERING EXERCISE

The centering exercise is presented in an outline form so that you may make an audio recording of the script as a guide. If you make a recording, be sure to speak in a soft and slow manner, allowing adequate pauses between steps. Once you have learned to complete each step from memory, you are advised to stop using the recording. After you have demonstrated the ability to successfully practice this exercise without a recording, it is recommended that you practice it once or twice a day for two weeks before continuing. If you are unable to practice at least five days per week, then extend the number of weeks accordingly before you proceed to the next exercise.

1. Sit in a comfortable and erect position in a chair or on the floor, facing east. Close your eyes and simply focus on your breath naturally flowing in and out. Do not count it or interfere with it in any manner.

2. After several breaths, say a short prayer invoking the aid of Deity, as you were taught when initiated as an Entered Apprentice.

3. After the prayer, begin to breathe rhythmically, as described in Exercise 1:10 of the *Breath* section. Complete seven cycles of rhythmic breathing.

4. Now focus your attention exclusively on the outer surface of your left ear for several seconds.

5. Once you have achieved a good focus on your left ear, allow your attention to expand, including the left side of your head and jaw, and your left eye. Allow the muscles in these areas to relax.

6. After several seconds, expand your awareness to include the left side of your neck and throat, feeling the area relax. Be sure your awareness is inclusive of your left ear and the rest of the left side of your face, all comfortably relaxed. You may notice a warm, tingly feeling as the blood flow increases in these areas.

7. After several seconds, shift your attention to the outer surface of your right ear for several seconds. As you do so, you may notice sensations that suggest a shift of energy from your left to your right.

8. Once you have achieved a good focus on your right ear, allow your attention to expand, including the right side of your head and jaw, and your right eye. Allow the muscles in these areas to relax.

9. Now allow your attention to focus for a minute in the very center of your head where right and left meet. Feel the energy shift to the center and a deep sense of relaxation and warmth at that point.

10. Move your focus to your left hand for several seconds. Allow the muscles to relax. As you do so, you may notice sensations that suggest a shift of energy to your left.

11. Expand your awareness to include your left arm and shoulder. Allow these muscles to relax.

12. After several seconds, include the left side of your chest and back. Allow these muscles to relax. You may notice a warm, tingling feeling in your left hand, arm, shoulder, chest, and back as the blood flow increases in these areas.

13. After several seconds, shift your attention to your right hand, and then repeat steps 10, 11, and 12 for that side of your upper body. As you do so, you may notice sensations that suggest a shift of energy from your left to your right.

14. Now allow your attention to focus for a minute in the very center of your chest where right and left meet. Feel the energy shift to the center and a deep sense of relaxation and warmth at that point.

15. Move your focus to the top of your left hip for several seconds. Allow the muscles to relax. As you do so, you may notice sensations that suggest a shift of energy to your left.

16. Expand your awareness to include the left side of your lower abdomen and your left buttock. Allow these muscles to relax.

17. After several seconds, include your left leg and foot. Allow these muscles to relax. You may notice a warm, tingling feeling in your left hip, lower abdomen, buttock, leg, and foot as the blood flow increases in these areas.

18. After several seconds, shift your attention to the top of your right hip, and then repeat steps 15, 16, and 17 for that side of your lower abdomen. As you do so, you may notice sensations that suggest a shift of energy from your left to your right.

19. Now allow your attention to focus for a minute in the very center of your lower abdomen where right and left meet. Feel the energy shift to the center and a deep sense of relaxation and warmth at that point.

20. Imagine an internal plumbline of brilliant white light running into the top of your head from the highest heavens, and down through your body into the depths of the Earth. Try to feel the presence of this plumbline as a magnetic or electrical current flowing between Heaven and Earth.

21. As you focus on the plumbline, allow it to grow in diameter so that it becomes a column of light with a circumference as large as your own head. Feel the pure white light as a warm, relaxing, cleansing, and healing energy.

22. Once the column of light is well established, exhale fully, imagining that the energy within the light is swirling down through your head and body, into the earth below. As you inhale fully, imagine that the energy is swirling up around and through your body into the heavens above. The swirling motion is from left to front to right to rear. Inhale and exhale with the same rhythm you used in step 3. Repeat this process seven times.

23. After the seventh breath, simply breathe naturally and take several minutes to work with the *Initial Contemplation* (see below).

24. After your contemplation, allow the imagery to fade, return your focus to your breath, and breathe rhythmically as in step 3. After seven cycles of inhale-exhale, open your eyes, clap your hands three times, and you are finished.

THE INITIAL CONTEMPLATION

As you focus on the column of light, contemplate the three principal supports of the Lodge - the pillars of Wisdom, Strength, and Beauty. Imagine that your column of light is the pillar of Beauty, while an immense bronze pillar of Wisdom is to your left and an equally large bronze pillar of Strength to your right. As a Mason, you know the names of the two bronze pillars are *Jachin* and *Boaz*. Imagine that all three pillars extend from the foundations of the

Earth to the canopy of Heaven. Consider the relationships among these three qualities. Make appropriate notes in your journal.

METHODS OF CONTEMPLATION

It should be noted that, in different traditions, the word "contemplation" can mean different things. For our purposes, it refers to our attempts to gain insight and understanding about a particular subject. There are three basic approaches that you may use in contemplation, and we refer to them as *associative*, *analytic*, and *intuitive*. Of course, no complex breathing techniques or meditations are necessary to use these methods of contemplation. However, such procedures do increase the potential benefits. You are advised to use only one form of contemplation per session, but to eventually use all three forms for each subject you choose. You may discover a particular order that seems most productive for you.

Associative contemplation continues to roll the subject around in the mind, examining every aspect of it, while attempting to make as many mental, emotional, and sensory associations as possible. In effect, it is a brainstorming technique. This type of contemplation draws together one concept or image with others, following all sorts of tangents, yet consistently returns to the central subject. It is, therefore, also a comparative technique and a useful tool for finding parallels and points in common between Masonry and other traditions. If you are currently following a specific religious, spiritual, or philosophical tradition, then you are encouraged to consider how Masonry compliments that tradition. Of course, the more you learn about psychology, philosophy, mythology, and religion, the more associations you will be able to form. In turn, the formations of these associations often reveal perspectives and possibilities that might have otherwise gone unnoticed.

Analytic contemplation uses logic and reasoning to break a subject down into its various parts and examine them closely, reducing each to an essential meaning. In a process not unlike mathematics, the significance of each part is added to that of the others. The end product is a greater appreciation of the whole, as well as deeper understanding of the details that make up the whole.

With intuitive contemplation, the goal is to still and quiet the mind as much as possible, while maintaining a focus on the subject. This quieting of the mind can be compared with settling the dust within a quarry. The method attempts to keep the subject at the center of an otherwise empty space in the mind. It avoids consciously analyzing or forming associations. At first, this may seem difficult, and it will suffice to continually and patiently redirect your mind back to the subject. It may be also be useful to formulate a word or phrase representing the subject, and then keep mentally repeating that word or phrase in order to drive all other thoughts out of awareness. Likewise, an image of some sort may also be used, maintaining that image in the mind to the exclusion of all other images. With practice, you can develop the ability to hold the subject quietly and gently in your mind for long periods of time, with few or no distractions. It is often the case that nothing particularly noteworthy happens during this type of contemplation, but it is nonetheless a very useful and important tool. Instead of resulting in the kinds of understanding that often flow immediately from the other types of contemplation, this technique sometimes works like the planting of a seed deep within your mind and spirit. That seed may sometime later produce a blossom of insight while performing a different type of contemplation, in a dream, or when you least expect it. On the other hand, this technique may stimulate a sudden reception of intuition during the contemplation itself. In any case, you are advised to concern yourself with the proper execution, rather than the results of this technique.

"The Ceremony of our first degree, then, is a swift and comprehensive portrayal of the entrance of all men into, first, physical life, and second, into spiritual life.... The first degree is also eminently the degree of preparation, of self-discipline and purification." — W.L. Wilmshurst, The Meaning of Masonry

THE ENTERED APPRENTICE RITUAL AND SYMBOLS

You now possess the basic working tools of contemplative Masonry. If you have completed the previous exercises faithfully and sincerely, then you have developed proficiency with those tools that will shed much more light on any subject to which you may attend. However, our primary purpose, and the reason you acquired this book, is to reveal more light in Masonry. You may therefore begin applying those tools to the ritual and symbols of the Entered Apprentice degree. This section provides you with further instructions on how to accomplish this task.

EXERCISE 1:16 – PREPARATION

You are advised to attend the initiation of an Entered Apprentice as soon as possible. Before you arrive at the lodge or temple, perform the centering exercise. As your contemplation, formulate two or three questions about specific things in the ritual that you wish to understand more fully. Once you have the questions clearly in mind, you may pray for more light on the Entered Apprentice degree. After completing the centering exercise, write the questions in your journal. You can then go to lodge and practice mindful and prayerful behavior during the ritual. To help you maintain focus, do not arrive early and do not stay late. As soon as you arrive home, do the centering exercise, contemplating the ritual as a whole, or any of its many steps. After the centering exercise, make appropriate notes in your journal, responding to the questions you previously wrote. You are advised to repeat this process of contemplative attendance of the Entered Apprentice ritual more than once, and you may do so as often or as many times as you wish. After having completed the process a few times, you may also begin participating in the ritual, being especially mindful and prayerful in the role or roles you play.

EXERCISE 1:17 - INITIATION

This exercise requires you to be the candidate of an Entered Apprentice initiation in your imagination. It need only be done once, though it will require more than one session. It is recommended that you prepare yourself to imagine the primary officers of the ritual as characters from our legend. In other words, the Worshipful Master is King Solomon, the Senior Warden is King Hiram of Tyre, and the Junior Warden is Hiram Abif. The following guidelines for visualization are offered for their symbolic value, but other details of imagery can be suitable.

Visualize King Solomon as a tall man, whose eyes are filled with wisdom. He wears a simple, golden crown and the Worshipful Master's jewel and apron. As the Worshipful Master is associated with the sun rising in the east, it is fitting to visualize King Solomon wearing a robe in the bright colors of the sunrise — violet and vermilion.

King Hiram of Tyre is a large, powerfully built man. He wears the Senior Warden's jewel and apron. As the Senior Warden is associated with the setting sun in the west, it is fitting to visualize King Hiram wearing a robe in the dark colors of dusk – indigo and crimson.

Hiram Abif is a very handsome man of average build and stature. He wears the Junior Warden's jewel and apron. As the Junior Warden is associated with the sun at its zenith, it is appropriate to visualize Hiram Abif wearing a robe in the colors of the midday sky – sky blue and gold.

The Senior Deacon wears the proper jewel and apron, and also carries the staff of that office. It is recommended that you visualize the Senior Deacon as the historical figure in Masonry that you most admire and respect. It is helpful to choose one for whom you have a photograph or portrait. As this officer escorts you through the north, and the north is said to be a place of darkness, it is fitting to visualize the Senior Deacon wearing a robe in the colors of midnight – black dotted with silver.

You will also need to visualize a fifth Master Mason as the one who prepares and assists your entrance in the anteroom and is later charitable to you in the northeast corner. It is recommended that you visualize the one Mason who has personally assisted you most in your Masonic career. Symbolically speaking, it is this Mason who has most assisted you in crossing the threshold from profane darkness to the Light of Masonry. Therefore, it is fitting to visualize this figure wearing a robe in the colors of twilight – purple dotted with silver.

Although we have much specific detail for the primary roles mentioned above, throughout the degrees you may also find a need to visualize other characters. You may visualize them as you see fit. However, with the exception of the fifth role mentioned in the preceding paragraph, you are advised not to visualize any other characters in the form of a physically living Mason.

To actually perform this exercise, begin by doing the centering exercise. When you reach the step for contemplation, imagine yourself as the candidate going through the Entered Apprentice degree. Over a span of two or three days, you are advised to perform three separate sessions, each one corresponding to a phase of the ritual. For convenience you may choose to begin the first phase with entering the preparation room and continue through the obligation. Do not forget that you were blind in this phase, which means that the primary sensory experience was hearing. In the second phase, move from being brought to light to receiving the working tools and exiting the lodge room. The third phase encompasses your return to the lodge room and the lessons that you then received. In the third phase, imagine yourself clothed as an Entered Apprentice. In each phase, make every effort to imagine each of the key points that you would actually experience as the candidate. Perfection is not to be expected, and characters other than those already mentioned do not require the same level of detail.

After completing the exercise, make appropriate notes in your journal. Be sure to answer the following questions:

- What emotions did you experience? Note at which parts of the ritual you experienced those emotions most strongly.

- What parts of the ritual seemed most meaningful to you? Explain what thoughts they stimulated.
- What parts of the ritual seemed most difficult to fully understand?
- What parts seem to hold deeper and more profound meaning than you currently grasp?
- In which parts of the ritual did you sense the Divine presence most clearly?

EXERCISE 1:18 – INSTRUCTION

These exercises entail more thorough contemplation of the details of the ritual and symbolism of this degree. There are literally thousands of details and hundreds of significant points. However, you are asked to further contemplate those parts you found most intriguing and inspiring in the previous exercise, as well as the key elements presented in this subsection. In addition to specifying those elements, this subsection will introduce you to a new type of contemplation.

The following list presents the key elements of ritual and symbolism for contemplation. You may make omissions or changes to reflect the details of your jurisdiction's ritual. As you complete a session for each element, be sure to make appropriate entries in your journal on the significance that each holds for you *at all four levels* of your psyche, especially relating to whatever religious, spiritual, or philosophical tradition that you personally follow. It is very important that you contemplate not only the teachings concerning each element, but the associated symbols and images as well.

1. The Three Distinct Knocks
2. The Conditions of Entrance
3. The Reception
4. The Role of the Senior Deacon
5. Psalm 133
6. The Circumambulations
7. The Obligation
8. Genesis 1:1-3
9. The Great Lights in the Entered Apprentice Degree
10. The Lesser Lights
11. The Due Guard, Penal Sign, and Step of the Entered Apprentice
12. The Word of the Entered Apprentice
13. The Lambskin as worn by the Entered Apprentice
14. The Northeast Corner
15. The Working Tools of the Entered Apprentice
16. The Situation and Form of the lodge
17. The Ornaments
18. The Principal Supports
19. The Covering of the Lodge and Jacob's Ladder
20. The Moveable Jewels
21. The Immovable Jewels
22. The Point Within the Circle Bordered by Parallel Lines
23. The Principal Tenets

24. The Four Points of Initiation and the Cardinal Virtues
25. Chalk, Charcoal, and Clay

In developing your understanding of each of these elements, you are advised to use the three basic types of contemplation within the context of the centering exercise. In addition, you should also begin using another type of contemplation, which is called *interactive*. It is recommended that you practice interactive contemplation no more than twice per week. Altogether, each element of the previous list should be worked on for at least a few days, completing no more than two per week. Depth of understanding for each element is always more important than the speed with which you advance to the next. Indeed, you will find that many elements continue to reveal their depths over years of contemplation. Be patient and use your best judgment before moving from one element to the next.

Interactive contemplation involves immersing yourself in the imagery of the chosen subject and having imaginary interaction and conversation with the characters involved. Now, there is indeed a bit of humor in the prospect of intentional daydreaming, and you could hardly be blamed for a chuckle or two as you read this paragraph. On the other hand, you may be taken aback and experiencing a little anxiety. Both of these responses are actually quite healthy. A little skepticism and caution never hurt anyone. However, this is serious business and you need only recall the previous exercise to see that you have already interacted with imaginary characters. The only difference now is that what you and the characters say and do will not be predetermined by the ritual.

How could it be helpful to have such imaginary interactions? Depth psychology and mystical religion have both acknowledged that the human psyche employs and responds to archetypal images. Simply stated, an archetypal image is a mental form that personifies a particular aspect or process of the psyche or of Nature. Carl Jung constructed an effective and well-respected system of psychotherapy incorporating the idea of archetypes. Hundreds of years ago, St. Ignatius of Loyola produced an entire system of Christian devotion based upon interacting with such images, and that system is still in use by the Jesuits. Furthermore, many mainstream and orthodox religions make use of archetypal images in the form of icons that serve as focal points for prayer and as reminders of saints and prophets who embodied some spiritual quality. Archetypal images can be found in mythic literature as the gods and goddesses of the ancient world. Archetypes also often appear in our dreams disguised in the images of the people we know and have read about or seen in movies.

The way these images work in our minds is somewhat mysterious, but we do know that they often serve as conduits for wisdom and understanding. In dreams and spiritual visions, such images can speak and act as though they have minds of their own. In fact, it is taught in many traditions that when an image has the proper form, the power or intelligence that it represents will actually inhabit it. In any case, our interest is in using such methods because they have been proven as effective means to gain more wisdom and understanding.

It should also be clear that we are not practicing a form of mental idolatry, as we will not be worshipping or praying to such images as though they are gods.

In order to work successfully with interactive contemplation, you need to start with a basic awareness of what the archetypal Masonic images personify. The image of King Solomon is, of course, an archetypal image of one granted wisdom and authority by God. In your psyche, his image speaks with the voice of spirit, intuition, creativity, and will. Hiram Abif is an archetypal image of one gifted with great knowledge and skill. In your psyche, his image speaks with the voice of intellect, reason, and balanced judgment. King Hiram of Tyre is an archetypal image of one possessed with great power and resources. In your psyche his image speaks with the voice of emotion and desire. The Senior Deacon is an archetypal image of a guide, one who instinctively knows the path you are following. In your psyche, his image speaks with the voice of the physical, of sensations, and behavior.

Before we go much farther, we should examine an apparent discrepancy. The hierarchy of the officers may not seem to precisely fit with the hierarchy of the psyche. In other words, Hiram Abif, the third officer, represents the second level of the psyche (intellect), while King Hiram, the second officer, represents the third level of the psyche (emotions). This discrepancy is resolved by considering the roles of emotion and the sources of desire. The role of emotion, like King Hiram, is to supply the energy and ability to actually accomplish labor. In short, emotion motivates the fulfillment of some desire. Whatever the nature of our desires, the fact remains that the body will do nothing, no matter how much intellectual sense an action may hold, unless there is energy available to drive it. Thus, from the perspective of actually doing something, the energy of emotion does take precedence over the designs of the intellect. Masonry is, after all, about making real differences in the material world. Still, the intellect remains at the second level of the psyche's hierarchy, for it more fully comprehends the intentions of the spirit and is able to translate them into designs for labor.

To begin a session of interactive contemplation, perform the centering exercise. When you reach the step for contemplation, formulate a single question concerning some part of the ritual and symbolism of the Entered Apprentice degree that you want to understand more fully. Next, imagine yourself clothed in a white robe, wearing your apron as an Entered Apprentice. Visualize yourself standing at the closed inner door of a lodge room. Knock upon the door, listening to the knock reverberating into the depths of the Cosmos. You hear the knock returned, and the door opens to reveal an Entered Apprentice lodge at labor, with the four officers at their stations. Note the illuminated symbol above King Solomon (this varies in some jurisdictions). Step inside and close the door behind you. Advance to the altar, notice its arrangement, present yourself in due form, and see King Solomon responding in kind. At this time you should invoke the aid of Deity with a short, heartfelt prayer asking for more light.

After your prayer, advance by the north to the east and approach King Solomon, the Worshipful Master. Note the illuminated symbol above his head. Ask him your question, keeping in mind that if he responds it will be with the voice of your spirit. His responses may be brief offerings of wisdom and inspiration, or questions intended to push you toward deeper insight. Instead of speaking, he may even make some gesture or movement. In any case, do not be concerned if his response is enigmatic or difficult to comprehend. Whatever his response is, simply accept it, thank him, and continue clockwise to the south.

Approach Hiram Abif and ask him your question. You should also inform him about any response you were given by King Solomon. His answers may be analytical and rational in nature. He might ask questions of you, which you should attempt to answer with the same logic and balanced judgment that you may expect from him. You may also ask a few questions to gain greater clarity and understanding of what he is communicating. However, resist the temptation to engage in a lengthy dialogue. When you are ready, thank him and continue clockwise to the west.

Approach King Hiram of Tyre and ask him your question. You should also inform him of what happened in the east and in the south. His responses may be emotional in nature, expressing strong desires and convictions about the issue. Like King Solomon, he may say something or make a gesture or movement. He is not likely to ask any questions. Do not be surprised if he expresses more than one emotion or desire. He may even express emotions and desires that seem to be contrasting and conflicting with each other. You may ask him questions about why he feels the way he does. As an Entered Apprentice, you are working to subdue your passions, and that requires greater emotional awareness and understanding. Therefore, it is appropriate to spend more time with King Hiram than you did in the east or the south. When you are ready, thank him and continue clockwise to the north.

Approach the Senior Deacon and ask your question. You should also recount what transpired in the east, south, and west. This officer's responses may be focused on the physical world, with instruction on ways to physically experience or express the truth of what you are learning. Changes in the way you behave and live your life might be suggested. You may discuss any of these matters further if you desire. As an Entered Apprentice, one of your primary concerns is in learning how to work in the quarries of life. That concern places more importance on attending to the Senior Deacon. When you are ready, offer your thanks and return directly to the altar.

At the altar, express your gratitude with a short heartfelt prayer of thankfulness. After the prayer, excuse yourself in due form, seeing King Solomon respond accordingly. Once again, take note of the illuminated symbol above his head. Walk to the outer door, open it ,and pass through. Turn to face it as it you close it. Allow the imagery to fade and complete the last steps of the centering exercise. Make appropriate notes in your journal.

"The shadow is a moral problem that challenges the whole ego-personality, for no one can become conscious of the shadow without considerable moral effort. To become conscious of it involves recognizing the dark aspects of the personality as present and real. This act is the essential condition for any kind of self-knowledge, and it therefore, as a rule, meets with considerable resistance." — Carl Jung, The Portable Jung, "Aion: Phenomenology of the Self"

TO SUBDUE OUR PASSIONS

Speculative Masonry places great emphasis upon your moral behavior. However, it is one thing to *act* according to Masonic virtues, and yet another thing to have both our inner and outer lives governed by these principles. As a contemplative Mason, you will now work more closely with your emotions and learn more about the meaning of the phrase "subdue my passions." You will also practice techniques enabling you to exercise a deeper awareness of your emotions and to arrive at a greater sense of inner harmony and outward composure.

It should be noted that the word "passions" is used in our ritual rather than the word "emotions." Passions are emotional complexes, groups of emotions joined together in relation to a specific desire. Passions are those emotional complexes which well up from deep within our being, urging us toward the attainment of some desired object or outcome. When passions are unrestrained and ineffectively channeled, they can flood the body with feelings and the mind with thoughts and images that seem totally out of control. However, when subdued and kept within due bounds, they can serve as a powerful source of motivation and fortitude in working toward a worthwhile goal.

As previously stated, the word "subdue" can be misleading. In a Masonic context, the word more properly refers to *mastery* of our passions. In order to master your passions, you should not deny or suppress your feelings. Rather, you should develop an acute awareness and acceptance of your emotions. In so doing, you are better prepared to manage your passions more appropriately. Also, please keep in mind that the goal of Masonry is to make good men better, not perfect. Intolerance of your own humanity is not only unhealthy; it can quickly lead you to become intolerant of others.

EMOTIONAL AWARENESS AND MANAGEMENT

The most basic human emotions seem to fit into polar relationships. In other words, pleasant emotions can be paired with unpleasant emotions. Furthermore, we can see that between the poles in each pair of opposites, there is an entire spectrum of human sentiment. Consider the following examples:

Affection	Hatred
Attraction	Repulsion
Awe	Irreverence
Confidence	Fear
Graciousness	Anger
Gratitude	Ingratitude
Happiness	Sadness
Hope	Despair
Innocence	Remorse
Pride	Shame
Satisfaction	Frustration
Serenity	Anxiety

We tend to think of those emotions in the left-hand column as positive, and those in the right-hand column as negative. We should be careful of placing too much emphasis upon the terms "positive" and "negative," because in doing so it becomes far too tempting to deny or try to ignore the unpleasant emotions. Take, for example, a common situation that arises when someone asks an obviously angry person if he is angry. The angry man then denies it because he thinks it is wrong to be angry, he doesn't like the way it feels to be angry, he doesn't want to offend the other person, or he isn't acting in a particularly angry way. This kind of denial is based upon either ignorance or fear. In other words, he really is angry, but his lack of awareness or inability to manage the emotion prevents him from admitting it either to himself or someone else. The danger in this kind of denial is that such feelings can build up inside us to the point of becoming completely unmanageable.

Take a moment to reflect upon the pairs of emotions. It easily becomes apparent that many of the pleasant emotions can become unhealthy when taken to an extreme, and many of the unpleasant emotions are quite healthy at the proper place and time. Keeping this in mind helps us focus on balance as the key to a healthy emotional life, but even here, there is the possibility for misunderstanding. The balance that we seek is not an effort to maintain a static state midway between extremes. Rather, the balance we strive for is a dynamic and harmonious flow of healthy emotions back and forth between the extremes, as is fitting for the situation.

In monitoring our emotions, we rely heavily on the feelings associated with them. Emotions do indeed have an effect upon our bodies. A consideration of our common language hints at an important relationship between emotions and our physical feelings. Think for a moment about these phrases:

- "I have a gut feeling."
- "That makes me sick to my stomach."
- "It takes my breath away!"
- "That warms my heart."
- "I have a lump in my throat."

EXERCISE *1:19*

Practice this exercise once or twice a day. For each session, choose one pair of emotions as a focus for contemplation. Perform the centering exercise, and for your contemplation, begin to think about the pair of emotions that you chose. Focus on the unpleasant emotion. Do your best to feel that emotion very clearly. It may help to remember or imagine some occasion that stimulates that feeling. Allow the emotion to become strong enough that you clearly feel it in your body. Be mindful of this experience and try to determine where in the body that emotion seems to be centered. Then allow the emotion to fade away. Focus once again on your breath flowing in and out in a natural rhythm. As soon as you feel calm again, begin to focus on the pleasant emotion from the chosen pair. Repeat the same process that you followed for the unpleasant emotion. Then allow the emotion to fade a little as you return your focus to your breath flowing in and out in a natural rhythm. Complete the centering exercise, and you are finished. You are also advised to be more mindful of your emotions during your daily activities. Pay close attention to exactly where and how you feel the different emotions in your body. Make notes in your journal. You may continue to the next exercise after you have worked at least twice with every pair of emotions.

EXERCISE *1:20*

Perform the same procedures as in the previous exercise, with the following exceptions. After a brief focus on the unpleasant feeling, contemplate how this emotion could be good and healthy. Notice how the energy changes as you direct your thoughts in this way. Imagine ways that its energy might be harnessed by you for constructive purposes. Next, focus on the pleasant feeling and contemplate how this emotion could become extreme and unhealthy. Finally, contemplate how these two emotions can interact in a harmonious way that contributes most to the wellbeing of others and you. In your daily activities, be especially mindful of how the energy of your emotions, both pleasant and unpleasant, can be employed in healthy, constructive ways. Be mindful of how that energy can be used in unhealthy, destructive ways, or simply wasted. Make notes in your journal. You may continue to the next exercise after you have worked at least once with each pair of emotions.

VICES AND VIRTUES

The title of this subsection draws your attention to another perspective on the passions. As you have experienced in the previous exercises, it is not necessarily how pleasant or unpleasant an emotion is that is particularly important. It is most important that you manage your emotions well and take advantage of their energy for constructive and healthy purposes. You have also been informed that passions are not simple emotions, but powerful emotional complexes.

The terms *vice* and *virtue* speak to how well the passions are managed. Passions, poorly managed, lead to behaviors and attitudes that collectively form a vice. Passions, properly managed, lead to behaviors and attitudes that collectively form a virtue. By discovering the defining characteristics of thought and behavior in the virtues, we can employ them in our lives, thus "divesting our minds and consciences of all the vices and superfluities of life."

There is an ancient tradition of seven fundamental pairs of vices and virtues, and you will use them as your guide for the following exercise. Four of these virtues are known as the *cardinal virtues*, and three as the *theological virtues*. The Entered Apprentice degree teaches about the cardinal virtues and, in some Masonic jurisdictions, has the three theological virtues as the principal rungs of Jacob's Ladder. The seven virtues are presented below. On the table, note the vices you would assign to each virtue.

Virtues	Vices
Charity	
Hope	
Faith	
Prudence	
Fortitude	
Temperance	
Justice	

EXERCISE *1:21*

To make use of this information, complete the following exercise. Once or twice a day, choose one pair of virtue and vice for contemplation within the centering exercise. Before the exercise, review the Masonic definitions of these virtues as well as definitions of the vices. Memorize them if you wish. During your contemplation, try to understand each more fully. Spend at least three sessions per pair. As you move through your daily activities, be mindful of the vices and virtues and of how you display both. Make notes in your journal answering the following questions:

- How have you displayed this vice and this virtue? What are some specific examples?
- What emotions are involved in the vice and in the virtue?
- How do you work through the unpleasant feelings you have - such as anger, remorse, shame, frustration, and sadness - when you realize you have committed this vice?
- How do you reward or encourage yourself for this virtue?
- Why is this virtue important?
- Why are this vice and virtue paired with each other?
- What are some ways that you could change the temptations for this vice into motivations for the virtue?

"You will thus perceive, Brethren, that the F.C. degree, sometimes regarded by us as a somewhat uninteresting one, typifies in reality a long course of personal development requiring the most profound knowledge of the mental and psychical side of our nature. It involves not merely the cleansing and control of the mind, but a full comprehension of our inner constitution, of the more hidden mysteries of our nature and of spiritual psychology."

W.L. Wilmshurst, *The Meaning of Masonry*

THE INNER WORK OF
A FELLOW CRAFT

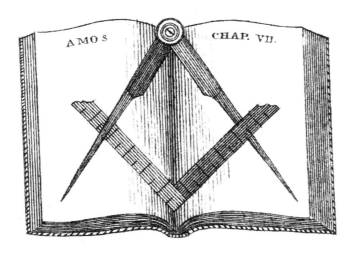

"The Ritual runs that our ancient brethren of this Degree met in the porchway of King Solomon's Temple. This is a way of saying that natural philosophy is the porchway to the attainment of Divine Wisdom; that the study of man leads to knowledge of God, by revealing to man the ultimate divinity at the base of human nature. This study or self-analysis of human nature Plato called Geometry..."
— W.L. Wilmshurst, *The Meaning of Masonry*

THE FELLOW CRAFT RITUAL AND SYMBOLS

There are no new methods to learn before you begin working in the Fellow Craft degree. In this section, you are given reminders on what techniques to apply, as well as a list of the key elements for contemplation.

EXERCISE 2:1 – PREPARATION

You are advised to attend the passing of a Fellow Craft as soon as possible. Before you arrive at the lodge or temple, perform the centering exercise. As your contemplation, formulate two or three questions about specific things in the ritual that you wish to understand more fully. Once you have the questions clearly in mind, you may pray for more light on the Fellow Craft degree. After completing the centering exercise, write the questions in your journal. You can then go to lodge and practice mindful and prayerful behavior during the ritual. To help you maintain focus, do not arrive early and do not stay late. As soon as you arrive home, do the centering exercise, contemplating the ritual as a whole or any one of its many steps. After the centering exercise, make appropriate notes in your journal, responding to the questions you previously wrote. You are advised to repeat this process of contemplative attendance of the Fellow Craft ritual more than once, and you may do so as often or as many times as you wish. After having completed the process a few times, you may also begin participating in the ritual, being especially mindful and prayerful in the role or roles you play.

EXERCISE 2:2 – PASSING

This exercise requires you to be the candidate of a Fellow Craft's passing. It need only be done once, though it will require more than one session. To actually perform this exercise, begin by doing the centering exercise. When you reach the time for contemplation, imagine yourself as the candidate going through the Fellow Craft degree. Over a span of two or three days, you are advised to perform three separate sessions, each one corresponding to a phase of the ritual. For convenience, you may choose to begin the first phase with entering the preparation room and continue through the obligation. Do not forget that you were blind in this phase, which means that the primary sensory experience was hearing. In the second phase, move from being brought to light to receiving the working tools and exiting the lodge room. The third phase encompasses your return to the lodge room and the lessons that you then received. In the third phase, imagine yourself clothed in a white robe, with the Fellow Craft apron. In each phase, make every effort to imagine each of the key points that you would actually experience as the candidate. Perfection is not to be expected, and characters other than those already mentioned do not require the same level of detail.

After completing the exercise, make appropriate notes in your journal. Be sure to answer the following questions:

- What emotions did you experience? Note at which parts of the ritual you experienced those emotions most strongly.

- What parts of the ritual seemed most meaningful to you? Explain what thoughts they stimulated.
- What parts of the ritual seemed most difficult to fully understand?
- What parts seem to hold deeper and more profound meaning than you currently grasp?
- In which parts of the ritual did you to feel the Divine presence most clearly?

EXERCISE 2:3 – INSTRUCTION

These exercises entail more thorough contemplation of the details of the ritual and symbolism of this degree. There are literally thousands of details and hundreds of significant points. However, you are asked only to further contemplate those parts you found most intriguing and inspiring in the previous exercise, as well as the key elements presented in this subsection.

The following list presents the key elements of ritual and symbolism for contemplation. You may make omissions or changes to reflect the details of your jurisdiction's ritual. As you complete a session for each element, be sure to make appropriate entries in your journal on the significance that each holds for you at all four levels of your psyche, especially relating to whatever religious, spiritual, or philosophical tradition that you personally follow. It is very important that you contemplate not only the teachings concerning each element but the associated symbols and images as well.

1. The Conditions of Entrance
2. The Reception
3. Amos 7:7-8
4. The Circumambulations
5. The Obligation
6. The Three Great Lights in the Fellow Craft Degree
7. The Due Guard, Penal Sign, and Step of the Fellow Craft
8. The Password of the Fellow Craft
9. The Apron of the Fellow Craft
10. The Working Tools of the Fellow Craft
11. Operative and Speculative Masonry
12. Boaz and Jachin
13. The Adornments of the Pillars
14. The Terrestrial and Celestial Globes
15. The Winding Staircase
16. The First Three Steps
17. The Five Orders of Architecture
18. The Five Human Senses
19. The Seven Liberal Arts and Sciences
20. The Emblem of Plenty
21. The Word of the Fellow Craft
22. The Wages of the Fellow Craft
23. The Letter G

In developing your understanding of each of these elements, you are advised to use all four types of contemplation – associative, analytical, intuitive, and interactive – within the context of the centering exercise. It is recommended that you practice the interactive form no more than twice per week. Altogether, each element of the previous list should be worked on for at least a few days, completing no more than two per week. Depth of understanding for each element is always more important than the speed with which you advance to the next. Indeed, you will find that many elements continue to reveal their depths over years of contemplation. Be patient and use your best judgment before moving from one element to the next.

To begin a session of interactive contemplation, perform the centering exercise. When you reach the step for contemplation, formulate a single question concerning some part of the ritual and symbolism of the Fellow Craft degree that you want to understand more fully. Next, imagine yourself clothed in a white robe, wearing your apron as a Fellow Craft. Visualize yourself standing at the closed outer door of a lodge room. Knock upon the door, listening to the knock reverberating into the depths of the Cosmos. You hear the knock returned, and the door opens to reveal a Fellow Craft lodge at labor with the four officers at their stations. Note the illuminated symbol above King Solomon. Step inside and close the door behind you. Advance to the altar, notice its arrangement, present yourself in due form, and see King Solomon respond in kind. At this time you should invoke the aid of Deity with a short heartfelt prayer asking for more light.

After your prayer, advance by the north to east and approach King Solomon, the Worshipful Master. Note the illuminated symbol above his head. Ask him your question, keeping in mind that if he responds it will be with the voice of your spirit. Whatever his response is, simply accept it, thank him, and continue clockwise to the south.

Approach Hiram Abif and ask him your question. You should also inform him about any response you were given by King Solomon. His answers may be characterized by reason and balanced judgment. You may also ask a few questions to gain greater clarity and understanding of what he is communicating. As a Fellow Craft, you have more of an emphasis on intellect. Therefore, you are encouraged to spend more time with Hiram Abif than you did as an Entered Apprentice. When you are ready, thank him and continue clockwise to the west.

Approach King Hiram of Tyre and ask him your question. You should also inform him of what happened in the east and in the south. His responses may be emotional in nature, expressing strong desires and convictions about the issue. You may ask him questions about why he feels the way he does. When you are ready, thank him and continue clockwise to the north.

Approach the Senior Deacon and ask your question. You should also recount what transpired in the east, south, and west. This officer's responses may be focused on the physical world with instruction on ways to physically experience or express the truth of what you are learning. Because of the change in priorities with this degree, you need not spend as much time with the Senior Deacon. When you are ready, offer your thanks and return directly to the altar.

At the altar, note the arrangement of the Three Great Lights. You should then express your gratitude with a short, heartfelt prayer of thankfulness. After the prayer, excuse yourself in due form, seeing King Solomon respond accordingly. Once again take note of the illuminated symbol above his head. Walk to the outer door, open it, and pass through. Turn to face it as it you close it. Allow the imagery to fade and complete the last steps of the centering exercise. Make appropriate notes in your journal.

"Man in the world of action loses his centering in the principle of eternity if he is anxious for the outcome of his deeds, but resting them and their fruits on the knees of the Living God he is released by them, as by a sacrifice, from the bondages of the sea of death." — Joseph Campbell, The Hero With a Thousand Faces

THE SECRET SMILE

As you know, the Fellow Craft degree continues the work that was begun in the Entered Apprentice degree. In that degree, emphasis was placed upon moral behavior and the healthy management of emotions. In this degree, more emphasis is placed upon refining the powers of the mind and executing judgment that is plumb, level, and square. It can be difficult to exercise such judgment when one is consciously preoccupied with managing and examining his or her emotions. Clearly, it would be desirable to have a greater ability to achieve the compassionate understanding that is the basic condition of sound judgment. This section will provide you with a method to accomplish that goal.

Think of all the positive conditions that a smile can communicate: happiness, satisfaction, amusement, peace, affection, hope, gratitude, and many other beautiful conditions of the human heart and mind. The state of equanimity can also be communicated by a smile. It is that peaceful little grin you often see on the faces of sages. When we see that smile, it communicates the sense of serenity and balance that accompanies a profoundly deep awareness of oneself, others, and the situation in the present setting. Those people who bear a genuine smile of this nature are able to think and act with great patience, honesty, understanding, and wisdom.

The technique that is offered in this section is called the Secret Smile. If you will recall, we are using a model of the psyche that begins at the top with the spiritual and reaches through the mental and emotional to the physical level. Using the Secret Smile, motivated by a spiritual aspiration for more balanced judgment, you make a decision and take action to change your emotional and mental state. The imagination enacts that decision. Then the physical body responds to that action with physiological and biochemical processes that actually change the way you feel. As your emotions become more peaceful and harmonious, your mind is cleared and freed to achieve deeper understanding and better judgment.

EXERCISE 2:4

It is recommended that you do the Secret Smile at least once a day. It is a good practice to perform it first thing in the morning before rising from bed, at noon, and just before you fall asleep. However, it is not always necessary to do all steps of the exercise to get some benefit from it. In situations where there isn't sufficient time or privacy, you can eliminate many of the steps, including closing your eyes. In fact, simply combining the smile itself with mindful and prayerful awareness can provide significant results, especially if you are regularly practicing the full technique of the Secret Smile. Throughout your day, you can probably find all kinds of opportunities to take just a minute or two to do some variation on the Secret Smile, even while there are other people around you. However, avoid any temptation to make these lesser versions the basis of your contemplative work. As always, continue to make appropriate notes in your journal.

1. Close your eyes, relax your belly, and simply focus on your breath naturally flowing in and out. Do not count it or interfere with it in any manner.

2. After you have relaxed a little, imagine your own face as though in a mirror. See that face smiling warmly.

3. Inhale and draw that image of your reflection into your own face, actually bringing its gentle warm smile to your face. Focus on the feeling of the smile in and around your mouth. There is an energy that accompanies a smile. Tune into that energy as it fills your face.

4. Now allow that energy to flow up to the center of your forehead. Focus on feeling the beautiful energy of the smile around your mouth and at that point in your forehead.

5. Now allow that energy to flow up over the top and back of your head, then down through your spine, across your anus and genitals, and up through your belly and solar plexus. Pay particular attention to the way the smile seems to naturally flow into and out of your heart as it returns to your face. Know and feel that the energy of the smile combines compassion with understanding. You may find it helpful to coordinate this circulation with your breath. Complete it at least seven times.

6. After the circulations, feel the energy of the smile in each part of your body, from the top of your head to the bottom of your feet. If you wish, play with the energy a little, moving more of it to one place or another in your body. Get used to manipulating it. If you have pain or discomfort anywhere in your body, you may be able to relieve it by concentrating the energy of the smile into that area.

7. After you have saturated your body with the smile, you may take some time to contemplate anything you wish. When you are ready to end the exercise, just return your attention to your breath naturally flowing in and out. After several breaths, open your eyes, and you are finished.

"....easy is the descent to Avernus: night and day the door of gloomy Dis stands open; but to recall thy steps and pass to the upper air, this is the task, this the toil!" — *Virgil, Aeneid, in Carl Jung's, The Portable Jung, "Individual Dream Symbolism in Relation to Alchemy"*

DREAMWORK

Dreams have been a source of intense interest and a focus for introspection for thousands of years. This section follows that tradition by presenting a basic theoretical perspective on dreaming, as well as methods of doing effective inner work with dreams. More specifically, this information will reveal how you can benefit from doing your own dream interpretations to gain deeper insight into yourself and your Masonic experience.

In the Fellow Craft degree, you have been encouraged to develop your mind. We tend to think of the mind as our conscious awareness. However, there is far more to the mind than we are ever entirely aware of at any given moment. Holistic maturation demands integrity, and integrity is the result of integration. Therefore, it is important to integrate the conscious and unconscious mind as much as possible, without breaking the due bounds of either. Dreamwork is a safe and time-tested method of performing such work.

Dreams have a significant potential for aiding holistic maturation, because dreaming is one of the psyche's methods of sorting out information, forming associations, and solving problems. Dreaming also serves as one of the means by which the unconscious mind communicates with the conscious mind. Therefore, involving your conscious awareness in this process actually establishes a dialogue between these two aspects of your psyche, ideally enabling you to become more whole and healthy.

Before getting into more detail about dreamwork, there are some precautionary considerations. Dreamwork can be very exciting and fantastic, rich with imagery and symbolism that may suggest all sorts of things. For some people, it can become tempting to believe that their deeper spiritual nature, or even God, is starting to speak to them or lead them solely through the language of their dreams. However, please note that your conscious mind is in the seat of authority with regard to your behavior. You were created for it to be so, and you should respect and maintain that arrangement. Always take the time to contemplate things from a rational and balanced perspective. An important tool for maintaining that balance is to share your dreams with at least one other person whom you can trust to be stable and well grounded. Explore different interpretations before you allow yourself to come to any conclusions.

While many of our dreams are not recalled and thus remain unconscious, some of our dreams are remembered and may, in fact, call upon the simultaneous participation of waking consciousness. In other words, sometimes we suspect or actually become aware that we are dreaming. We call that phenomenon *lucid dreaming*. Though there are methods for and rewards from developing one's capacity for lucid dreaming, the benefits from dreamwork are not limited to lucid dreaming. In fact, this lesson is not directly concerned with lucid dreaming, and it is suggested that you not begin any investigation or experimentation along those lines until after completing the work in this book.

In dreams we are often confronted with imagery that may be enthralling, titillating, confusing, threatening, or even horrifying. These experiences are sometimes so realistic and intense that we may not be able to distinguish them from our waking world. It's easy to see why the world of dreams might be thought of as a world of its own. After all, in dreams, unexpected events happen, and people act and speak without our conscious direction. In fact, according to the spiritual traditions of many cultures, the dream world is a real world, paralleling and interacting with the physical world, though operating according to different laws.

For our purposes, the dream world is a world of symbolism, mythology, and psychology. By examining the imagery, themes, and your emotional responses to your dreams, you can become aware of previously unknown conflicts or potentials in your own psyche. For example, a dream involving an argument between a man and a woman about finances might actually be symbolic of the dialogue between conflicting needs of stability and spontaneity in one's life, with the finances representing one's energy. Your reaction to the argument and characters would probably serve as a good starting place for reaching a more satisfactory balance between stability and spontaneity. The basic point is that remembered and lucid dreams can be a source of information about yourself which can, in turn, lead to greater wholeness and maturation.

INTERPRETING YOUR OWN DREAMS

You may already practice some specific form of dream interpretation. If you are satisfied with that, then you are welcomed to continue with it. In any case, you are encouraged to continue reading this section. There are many different schools of thought regarding dream interpretation. Some say dreams refer to the past, some say they are most relevant to the present, and others consider them a rehearsal or preparation for the future. Certain viewpoints rely on a complex archetypal symbology or a belief that all dream elements refer to specific instincts, drives, and ego defenses. Others begin with the assumption that dream symbolism is highly personal and flexible.

It seems reasonable to conclude that there is some truth to each of these positions. In fact, there is evidence to suggest that your dreams will conform to whatever method of interpretation you wish to practice. For these reasons, we assume that, ultimately, nobody can be more qualified than you to discover the meaning in your dreams, though input from others can be quite valuable. Once you begin to pay more attention to this dialogue between the conscious and unconscious, you will find your own characteristic patterns of imagery and symbolism. At times, these may clearly refer to unfinished business from the past. On other occasions, they may help you work out immediate issues or lead you into new directions for the future. More often than not, they speak to you on all these levels.

GENERAL GUIDELINES

When interpreting your dreams, try to remember a few important ideas. First, it is largely the interaction between the various aspects of your own psyche that is creating the dream. Second, dreams are usually highly symbolic. Third, interpretations can yield insights on personal, social, and spiritual levels.

It is very important to remember that your psyche and experiences supply the canvas and paints of your dreams. Even more importantly, it is within your unconscious mind that the brushes and strokes which put your dreams together are applied. This is important, because your dreams often involve people, places, and things that seem very familiar. Therefore, if you interact with your spouse, parent, or a close friend in your dream, remember that you most probably have not made psychic contact with the actual person. Rather, you have seen their image, an image provided by your own mind and experience. Likewise, dreams about demons or angels are far less likely to be interactions with such beings than they are interactions with threatening elements of your own psyche.

It is also important to remember that it is primarily your psyche that constructs whatever pleasures, pains, difficulties, or curiosities you may experience in a dream. For instance, if you have a dream about your spouse being unfaithful, it would be unfair to wake up and act with jealousy or suspicion toward your spouse. Instead, realize that this dream probably says more about you and your own fears than it does about your spouse. "Projection" is an important word to remember in this context, for we project our own emotions and desires onto the characters in our dreams just as a movie projector puts images on a screen.

This leads us to the second point: Try to uncover the hidden messages within your dreams. Although a dream may well be taken at face value, there may yet be more to it. Your unconscious mind often creates seemingly concrete imagery to help you experience and work out more abstract problems. In the preceding example, the dream of your spouse's affair might well be a symbol for the consequences that come from inattention to a deeper sense of meaning and purpose in one's life. In effect, the spouse could represent your spirit, which you have denied, and which is demanding more attention. The message could be that you need to work on a more intimate and nurturing relationship with your spirit and to stop playing a role that has been accepted from others. If this facade is allowed to continue, you might run the risk of losing touch with the gifts that make you a truly unique and valuable individual. On the other hand, the dream might simply be a reminder of your own insecurities in relationships. The key thing to remember is that dreams, just like any good story, usually have underlying themes and messages.

When you start trying to find a hidden meaning, try to be open to possibilities at all levels. In our ongoing example, there are both personal and social aspects to the dream. We have discussed much of what you might gain as personal insight. However, the dream may well speak about trouble that does in fact exist in the marriage. In another instance, perhaps in a dream of losing a race with your friends, your unconscious may be saying that you and your friends are creating a more competitive atmosphere than you would prefer. In short, remember that a human being is a creature living in both a private context and a social context, and these two dimensions continually interact, even in your dreams.

Finally, you are advised to keep in mind that balance is an important part of dream interpretation. It is very easy to interpret dreams as entirely bright and encouraging on the one hand or as completely dark and foreboding on the other. A single dream may have many layers of meaning, and like any good teacher, they often combine encouragement with critique.

AN INTERPRETIVE METHOD

Of course, it's quite easy to say that dreams are symbolic, and that all you need do is search out their hidden meanings. It is quite another to delve fully into all that symbolism and consistently come up with valid and useful insights. The method recommended by this book is comprised of examining the significant aspects of a dream from a subjective viewpoint. Subjectively examining dream elements means trying to understand each element's purpose from its own unique perspective. The way this interpretation is accomplished is through identifying oneself with the thing or character and then trying to verbalize its thoughts, feelings, functions, or purposes in the context of the dream.

As an example, consider a dream reported by "Nick." After recently ending a romantic relationship, Nick dreamt of walking down a hill with a large, heart-shaped vase. To gather more meaning from this dream, Nick closed his eyes and imagined he was the vase. He tried to physically feel like the vase. Nick asked himself, "What is my purpose? What does it mean that I am heart-shaped? Why am I being carried? Where am I going? How do I feel about this situation?"

Becoming fully involved in this work, Nick discovered some interesting answers: "As a vase, I receive pretty things like flowers, hold them for a while, and when they get old, I'm ready for something new. I'm heart-shaped, because I was a gift of love. I remind people that they were once loved. As the vase, I am being carried, because I must be given from one person to another and I can't be allowed in this person's chest like a real heart. I am going down this hill, from some place higher to some place lower. I feel sad for the one who is carrying me, because we are going down into a low place." These subjective reports helped Nick experience the grief he had been denying and avoiding since the break-up. It also suggested to him that he had a hidden bias toward believing that even the best relationships are only temporary, "pretty things" to be replaced "when they get old."

Let's examine a dream from "Ron," a new Master Mason and Junior Steward of his lodge. Ron had a strange nightmare in which an ugly green monster was biting off peoples' fingers while clicking a television remote. Ron tried to assume its identity. "Why am I ugly?

Why green? Why am I biting off peoples' fingers? Why am I clicking the remote?"

These were Ron's answers: "As the monster I am ugly, because I don't know how to be attractive, to be liked. I am green, because I am rotten and also because I am envious of the beauty and joy in other's lives. As the monster, I bite off people's fingers, because that way, their hands become useless. I click the remote, because I wish I could just change everyone's channel."

Ron followed this with the subjective views of a useless hand and the television remote: "As a useless hand, I can no longer point at anyone in blame. As the remote, I have no mind of my own. I only serve my master."

While working on his dream, Ron realized that he had recently been complaining to the Worshipful Master of his lodge about other brethren not seeming serious enough about their duties in the lodge. It then became apparent to him that he was envious of their ability to be relaxed and informal with each other, while he felt uptight and competitive. In effect, as the Junior Steward, Ron had begun to feel like the lodge's "remote control." He was also fearful that his brethren would point their fingers at him in the way that he had pointed his finger at them. The dream also revealed to Ron that he had a deep, mistaken belief that being meek and submissive is what it takes to be considered a good person. Interpreting the dream in this manner enabled Ron to relax and enjoy his duties as Junior Steward. His attitude and demeanor improved, leading him to establish better relationships with his brethren and feel more comfortable in the lodge.

Using this method of interpretation helps you establish your own dream vocabulary. Nobody can determine for you that a particular image has to mean a particular thing. Your personal thoughts, feelings, and life experiences determine which images your unconscious mind uses in its effort to work with your consciousness. Therefore, as you become more attentive to your dreams and more experienced at looking for their deeper meanings, your conscious and unconscious will learn how to relate with each other in a way that is especially natural and effective for you.

GETTING STARTED

There are two levels at which you can do effective dreamwork. You can choose to be very dedicated and make it a structured part of your life. On the other hand, you may prefer to rely on dream-work as an occasional contributor to your holistic maturation. In either case, you can reap significant rewards. The degree to which you work with your dreams is simply a matter of your own preferences and judgment. However, you are encouraged to at least record and contemplate those dreams that are especially vivid and memorable.

In order to make dreamwork a structured part of your life, you need to begin keeping your journal or a small tape recorder near your bed. You can then use your dreams, either freely or focused, as a means of gaining insight into particular issues. To work freely with your dreams you simply make notes on the basic information of every dream you recall from the previous night. Your basic notes might take the following form:

Where: A parking garage
When: At night, about 10:00, but it seemed like 20 years
*   ago, when I was a teen*
Who: Me, my best friend from that time, and an unknown
*   man*
What: Washing a red car together
Feelings: It felt good. We were working and having fun
*   together like old times*

This information requires only a minute or two of your time, yet provides you with enough clues for performing a full interpretation later that day. Before you begin your interpretation, you might want to write down a few more details. For instance, you might record the following:

The parking garage was very clean and empty. My best friend
and I never even spoke with each other. The unknown man
seemed like he might be the owner of the car. He just smiled
a lot and patiently watched us. The car was very nice and
plush. It was a four-door and had all the extras.

It would also be useful to review dreams of the previous few days to see if there are any recurring images or themes. You would now be ready to do an interpretation, including the subjective views for each element in the dream. As you did so, you would make whatever notes were necessary to formulate and record your understanding of the dream.

While structured dreamwork is a great tool for holistic maturation, it can be so time consuming as to interfere with your other duties. In fact, it may become somewhat draining because the intense focus on dreaming can interfere with natural sleep patterns. Therefore you may choose to only do occasional dreamwork of this nature, which can be quite rewarding. The difference with this method is that you only record notes and perform interpretations for dreams that are particularly vivid or intriguing. Again, it is helpful for you to look back over previous notes for recurring images and themes. You might find that a dream you just had could help you gain insight into an entire series of dreams spread out over months or even years.

An Alternative Method for Interpretation

The following technique may be easier for some persons and require less time, while also providing valuable experience in different states of consciousness. It is especially useful for vivid dreams. It is not unusual for vivid dreams to lead one directly from sleep to a state of consciousness that is between normal wakefulness and true dreaming. In this state, called *hypnopompia*, mental images and thoughts can continue to spontaneously arise, yet the dreamer is also conscious and aware of lying in bed, awakening from a dream. A similar state, *hypnogogia*, can also be induced by the dreamer attempting to slip back into a dream from which one has just started to awaken. You can take advantage of these in-between states for dream interpretation.

As you begin to awaken from a vivid dream, allow yourself to go back into it. It is not necessary to fall back into sleep. Rather, you can simply relax and slide into the hypnogogic state, attempting a visual remembrance of the dream. As you do this, mentally ask about the nature of the dream or any of its parts. Then just relax and wait for the answer. Often the response will be immediate and may be a feeling or an intuitive understanding. Sometimes a single word may suddenly come to mind that makes everything clear. Just remain open and trust that the answer will come to you. As with the other method, it is recommended that you keep notes in your journal.

A FINAL EXAMPLE

The following account recalls a dream experienced by a Mason, "Bob," who was involved in a program of holistic maturation, routinely practicing contemplation in addition to his dreamwork. This dream serves as a wonderful example of the results that serious dreamwork can produce. As you read the account, keep in mind all that you have learned about dream symbolism. Compare your thoughts to Bob's interpretation.

The dream occurred after almost two weeks of daily contemplation and prayer in which Bob was focused on the idea of the "Temple not made with hands." Bob was thinking of this Temple as a symbol of his whole psyche, but he was feeling out of touch with his spirit. Bob lacked a sense of connection with his spirit and with God. He acknowledged that he had been feeling spiritually lost for some time. His contemplations led him to believe that somehow the degrees of Masonry held a key to regaining this connection. Each day, he would study Masonic books that had a spiritual perspective on the Craft and practice about 15 to 30 minutes of contemplation. Each night before he went to sleep, Bob would pray that his dreams would help him make the progress he was seeking.

One night Bob had the following dream. He found himself standing in a small rock quarry with high cliffs all around him. He didn't feel endangered, but it did seem to him that there was no way out. He had the feeling that he was supposed to be working, that he had a lot to get done, but that he was behind in his work. Bob couldn't remember what it was he was supposed to do.

Bob started searching around the quarry, looking for some indication of what kind of work he should do. He found a rope tied around a stone block, and he could see that someone had been dragging it toward a pile of blocks on the other side of the quarry. Bob picked up the rope and dragged the block to the pile. As he arrived there, he noticed a mine entrance nearby in the face of the rock. He instantly found himself standing at the mine entrance where he saw a large, dirty, and sweaty man standing in the mine. The man was holding a lantern, and he motioned for Bob to follow him.

Bob felt wary of the man, but he also felt compelled to follow him. They kept going deeper into the mine, which grew darker with each step. Bob was feeling more and more frightened, and he started having trouble breathing. Finally, deep in the mine, the large man stopped and turned to look at Bob. The man smiled a big smile and held the lantern up to the wall at Bob's left. A skull was protruding from the wall, as though it had been buried there.

Bob now felt very scared. The large man told Bob to get the skull, but Bob didn't move. Bob heard a rumbling, and dust started to fall from the ceiling beams. The large man shouted at Bob to grab the skull. Bob still refused to move. The earth rumbled even more, and the ceiling beams began to groan. The large man reached up to support the beam over their heads. He glared at Bob furiously and cursed at him, ordering him to take the skull out of the wall. Bob was frozen with fear. The mine started to collapse around them and the large man just started laughing. He shouted, "Here we go again!" Then Bob awoke, gasping for breath, as it seemed he was being buried alive.

Bob concluded that this dream was an encounter with his own fears, and divided it into two stages. In the first stage, Bob realized that the quarry represented the psychological pit he had created for himself. Bob acknowledged that for too long he had ignored his feelings of being lost and disconnected from his spirit. Dragging the block was symbolic of his decision to start working, and he felt good that he had been able to find something constructive to do. Bob thought that the block was his "rough ashlar," and he saw it as a symbol of his life in the physical world. He had, in effect, dragged himself to a new place where he could refine himself with contemplation and dreamwork. Bob made note that there were other blocks in the pile, suggesting that he really wasn't alone in his effort. He realized that as he and others worked on their psyches in this way, they were indeed refining themselves as "living stones."

In the second phase of the dream, Bob decided that the image of large man had brought him face to face with his biggest fear. The man's appearance reminded Bob of his desire to avoid the dirtiness of his own psyche. Like many of us, Bob had never really allowed himself to think much about his "darker" side. However, the dirty man was also very strong. Bob knew this meant that he had strength within himself that he had not tapped. The man carried a lamp, which Bob interpreted as a sign that he was being shown something hidden, but very important. To Bob, the journey into the depths of the mine symbolized his own realization that he had to probe very deeply within his own mind to find the way out of the pit he had created for himself. As Bob reflected on this, he noted the similarity of the words "mine" and "mind."

The crisis point in the dream involved the image of a skull, which Bob immediately recognized as a symbol of death. Bob admitted that he had always been terrified by the thought of dying. He realized that he had long avoided spiritual studies because of that fear. In the dream, being frozen with fear had prevented him from grabbing the skull. Bob now realized that had he grabbed the skull as he had been told to do, then the mine would not have collapsed. He understood this to mean that until he fully accepted and worked with his fear of death, there would be no escape from the pit represented by the rock quarry. He also realized that he was no more than an apprentice as long as he remained in that pit. The large man's final words forced Bob to acknowledge that this fear had led to failure on many occasions. The man's laughter helped Bob to get a better appreciation for how absurd it was to be paralyzed by this fear.

Though this dream ended as a nightmare, Bob was very thankful for its message. After finalizing his interpretation, he felt a sense of relief as well as a greater sense of direction and purpose in his contemplative work. Today Bob reports that utilizing such practices in connection with his Masonic interests has been very rewarding in all aspects of his life.

Initial Assignment

The following assignment will provide you with a rudimentary experience in dreamwork. First, choose one symbol or teaching from either of the first two degrees, one that seems to you to be particularly interesting or mysterious. For one or two weeks, as you fall asleep each night, mentally repeat the following phrase: "My dreams will teach me about how _____ fits into my life." Fill in the blank with the thing you have chosen. Consider expressing your desire in the form of a prayer before you go to sleep. When you awaken, record in your journal whatever you recall of your dreams. At some point, perform the centering exercise or the Secret Smile and carefully contemplate how the imagery and events of your dream might reveal more light on the symbol or teaching that you are studying. You may use all the tools of contemplation that you have been practicing. At some point, you will feel that you have received sufficient information to coordinate your experiences into a meaningful statement of deeper understanding regarding the symbol or teaching. At that point, write a thorough explanation of your understanding and share it with another Mason. After completing this assignment, use your own judgment about the extent to which you will make dreamwork a part of your contemplative pursuits.

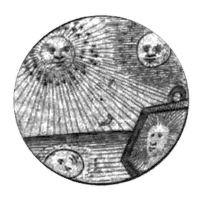

"*The Rosicrucians declared that the material arts and sciences were but shadows of the divine wisdom, and that only by penetrating the innermost recesses of Nature could man attain to reality and understanding.*" — *Manly P. Hall, The Secret Teachings of All Ages*

To Polish and Adorn the Mind

As a Speculative Fellow Craft, you learned that study of the seven liberal arts and sciences is recommended for its tendency to polish and adorn the mind. However, it is clear that our ancient brethren intended something other than mere academic education. Instead, the arts and sciences are used to draw our attention to the importance of intellectual development within a context of spiritual and moral principles. In this section, you will be presented with suggestions on how you can polish and adorn your mind in a more contemporary way that is consistent with the ancient tenets of Masonry.

To persons of the seventeenth and eighteenth century, it might have seemed that a broad distribution of knowledge and academic instruction would ensure the elevation of moral and spiritual enlightenment throughout civilization. In the present era, almost the entire population of the free world has access to education in the arts and sciences. However, frequently we find that the spiritual and the scientific seem to be in great conflict. Intellectual enlightenment sometimes produces more agnosticism, and even atheism, than it does reverence and inspiration. Conversely, religious devotion often takes an anti-intellectual position that ignores the theories and discoveries of science. Still, Masonry continues to claim that polishing and adorning the mind is beneficial to our purposes.

With good reason, geometry is distinguished from all the arts and sciences as the basis of Masonry. It is said that geometry reveals the handiwork of Divine Intelligence in the proportions, symmetry, and order of nature, and that we are to imitate these designs in our thoughts and behavior. We learn that virtuous behavior depends upon keeping our passions within due bounds, which in turn depends upon the application of reason and good judgment. This alignment of the intellect over the emotions and the body results in a life that more closely reflects the natural order established by the Creator. However, the intellect is not the apex of that order.

While the mind may use its great powers to understand the natural world, it is misleading to do so without consideration of a Supreme Being that makes it possible for the natural world to exist. Such purely materialistic thinking leads to the perception that the universe is essentially a great cosmic accident. In this view, life and intelligence are mere byproducts of matter. It is then a very short intellectual step to decide that the value of human life, much less moral behavior, is simply arbitrary. Obviously, such thinking is in conflict with Masonic teachings.

Every Mason knows that his first duty is to God. In fact, every lesson of Masonry includes reverence for the Creator as the very source from which light and life emanate. This practice acknowledges the Divine as both the foundation and the apex of all order and design. Thus Masonry recognizes the proper hierarchy of the human psyche as the spiritual over the intellectual, the intellectual over the emotional, and the emotional over the physical. Therefore, the intellectual studies of Masons should strengthen and support their reverence and awe for the Grand Artificer of the Universe and inspire the continued search for more light. Accordingly, Masons most properly polish and adorn their minds when they pursue studies in the arts and sciences that mend the rift between science and spirituality.

Among the more advanced thinkers of both science and spirituality, there have always been those individuals who realized the harmony between these two approaches to truth, beauty, and justice. Today, there is a vigorously growing body of literature filling the gap between science and spirituality. Indeed, among those who delve most deeply into such matters, it is increasingly difficult to determine where spirituality begins and science ends.

The psychological appreciation of myth is one of the first fields in which the ancient spiritual teachings and modern science have been able to meet in agreement. As science has learned more about the human mind, the fanciful tales of gods, goddesses, heroes, and heroines have revealed greater depths of wisdom and understanding.

In times not too far removed, the prevailing view in the academic world was that the ancient myths were primitive attempts to explain the forces and workings of nature or to present moral and social lessons. However, as psychology turned its focus away from the laboratory and onto the great literature of the ancients, it saw that these tales are allegories that symbolically conceal and reveal the greatest mysteries of the human psyche and its development. The scientific students of humanity realized that across all boundaries of time, geography, and culture there have been certain symbols, themes, and archetypes that consistently emerge from behind the various masks of our myths. They discovered that the characters not only represented the elements, forces, and events "out there" in the natural and social world, but also those within the body, mind, and spirit of human beings.

Because Masonry is itself based upon such mythic symbolism, it follows that these discoveries hold a wealth of insight that is applicable in contemplation. When, in this light, we carefully examine the stories associated with the Temple builders, we can see that they too show us very specific patterns and plans for our work in holistic maturation. Each character in our stories can be understood as representing an aspect of the psyche and/or the Divine. Each event and set of circumstances is a symbolic commentary on the faculties and skills we must develop and employ as we seek to more fully integrate and actualize the physical, emotional, intellectual, and spiritual aspects of our being.

The "soft" science of psychology and its views on mythology do not alone account for the entire overlap of science and spirituality. As the "hard" sciences of biology, chemistry, and physics have continued to probe the material world, they have discovered limitations and unexpected events that have forced them in new directions. Increasingly, the cutting edge of science acknowledges that the physical world itself must be based upon a metaphysical reality. Beyond the experimental laboratory, scientists must rely upon logic and mathematics to make any sense of what they witness in the universe. They further discover that mathematical and logical skills alone are not enough, for they must in turn be guided by the unquantifiable faculties of imagination, intuition, creativity, and will. The most intrepid of these seekers of knowledge postulate that consciousness and intelligence may be fundamental principles of existence itself, rather than mere by-products of random material interactions. In the end, such scientists often find themselves in agreement with ancient mystical teachings about the nature of the Cosmos.

None of this should be any great surprise to a diligent student of Masonry and its contributing traditions. For more than three hundred years, the Craft has consistently taught that a careful investigation of Nature would reveal the handiwork of a Supreme Intelligence. Our wisest scientists have demonstrated this truth time and again throughout history. In fact, it may have been easier for the average person to grasp this truth in more distant times. Perhaps we did not have to look so hard for God when humanity was less preoccupied with the minutia of matter and less blinded by the notion that materialistic science could explain everything that one might experience. Nevertheless, today's Mason lives in a time when many people are still burdened by the conceits of materialistic science. It is therefore fitting for contemplative Masons to pursue studies that rend the intellectual veil of materialistic science, and by doing so, see for themselves how science can lead back to the mysteries of Spirit.

As a contemplative Mason, you are advised to engage in a study of the intellectual fields where science and spirituality meet. It is recommended that you perform this study by carefully reading and contemplating appropriate books. A beginning list has been provided in *Appendix B: Bibliography*, under the heading "On Science and Spiritual Psychology." Books of this nature can sometimes be difficult to read due to unfamiliar words and concepts. As you encounter those challenges, you are encouraged to take the time necessary to become familiar with such terms. Although an initial assignment is given here, it is expected that an ongoing and less formal study of such fields will become a regular part of your contemplative work.

INITIAL ASSIGNMENT

To begin your work in this important aspect of contemplative Masonry, you are advised to choose three books from the previously mentioned list, or other books of this nature. Taking one at a time, read each book carefully and highlight those sentences that most demand your attention. Use the centering exercise or the Secret Smile to contemplate the messages of the book. You should also contemplate how the knowledge you are gaining could be applied to your understanding of Masonry. Make appropriate notes in your journal. When you have finished the book, coordinate your various insights and write a thorough explanation of what you have learned and how it has affected your understanding of Masonry. Include specific examples and references to Masonic rituals, symbols, and teachings. This work should require several pages and may take a week or two to complete. Adherence to a formal essay structure is recommended but not necessary. When you have finished the writing, share it with at least one other Mason, asking for a candid response to your thoughts. As you discuss the work, do not avoid or resist any clear indications for changes in your thinking. Keep in mind that no intellectual understanding can ever completely do justice to the eternal mysteries. When you have completed the assignment for all three books, you may advance to the next chapter.

"And as in each Triangle of Perfection, one is three and three are one, so man is one, though of a double nature; and he attains the purposes of his being only when the two natures that are in him are in just equilibrium; and his life is a success only when it too is a harmony, and beautiful, like the great Harmonies of God and the Universe."

"Such, my Brother, is the True Word of a Master Mason; such the true ROYAL SECRET, which makes possible, and shall at length make real the HOLY EMPIRE of true Masonic Brotherhood"

Albert Pike, Morals and Dogma

THE INNER WORK OF
A MASTER MASON

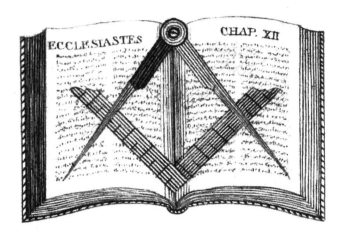

"*The Master who is at-one with both Nature and Divinity discerns the truth, and teaches and records it for all future generations of men.... but it should ever be remembered that the sole authority of the Master is in the Truth; and not the authority of Truth in the Master.*" — *J.D. Buck, Mystic Masonry*

THE MASTER MASON RITUAL AND SYMBOLS

There are no new methods to learn before you begin working in the Master Mason degree. In this section, you are given reminders on what techniques to apply, as well as a list of the key elements for contemplation.

EXERCISE 3:1 – PREPARATION

You are advised to attend the raising of a Master Mason as soon as possible. Before you arrive at the lodge or temple, perform the centering exercise. As your contemplation, formulate two or three questions about specific things in the ritual that you wish to understand more fully. Once you have the questions clearly in mind, you may pray for more light on the Master Mason degree. After completing the centering exercise, write the questions in your journal. You can then go to lodge and practice mindful and prayerful behavior during the ritual. To help you maintain focus, do not arrive early and do not stay late. As soon as you arrive home, do the centering exercise, contemplating the ritual as a whole, or any one of its many steps. After the centering exercise, make appropriate notes in your journal, responding to the questions you previously wrote. You are advised to repeat this process of contemplative attendance of the Master Mason ritual more than once, and you may do so as often or as many times as you wish. After having completed the process a few times, you may also begin participating in the ritual, being especially mindful and prayerful in the role or roles you play.

EXERCISE 3:2 – RAISING

This exercise requires you to be the candidate of a Master Mason's raising. It need only be done once, though it will require more than one session. To actually perform this exercise, begin by doing the centering exercise. When you reach the time for contemplation, imagine yourself as the candidate going through the Master Mason degree. Over a span of two or three days, you are advised to perform three separate sessions, each one corresponding to a phase of the ritual. For convenience you may choose to begin the first phase with entering the preparation room and continue through the obligation. Do not forget that you were blind in this phase, which means that the primary sensory experience was hearing. In the second phase, move from being brought to light to receiving the working tools and exiting the lodge room. The third phase encompasses your return to the lodge room and the lessons that you then received. In the third phase, imagine yourself clothed in a white robe, wearing the apron as a Master Mason. In each phase, make every effort to imagine each of the key points that you would actually experience as the candidate. Perfection is not to be expected, and characters other than those already mentioned do not require the same level of detail.

After completing the exercise, make appropriate notes in your journal. Be sure to answer the following questions:

- What emotions did you experience? Note at which parts of the ritual you experienced those emotions most strongly.
- What parts of the ritual seemed most meaningful to you? Explain what thoughts they stimulated.
- What parts of the ritual seemed most difficult to fully understand?

- What parts seem to hold deeper and more profound meaning than you currently grasp?
- In which parts of the ritual did you to feel the Divine presence most clearly?

EXERCISE 3:3 – INSTRUCTION

These exercises entail more thorough contemplation of the details of the ritual and symbolism of this degree. There are literally thousands of details and hundreds of significant points. However, you are asked only to further contemplate those parts you found most intriguing and inspiring in the previous exercise, as well as the key elements presented in this subsection.

The following list presents the key elements of ritual and symbolism for contemplation. You may make omissions or changes to reflect the details of your jurisdiction's ritual. As you complete a session for each element, be sure to make appropriate entries in your journal on the significance that each holds for you at all four levels of your psyche, especially relating to whatever religious, spiritual, or philosophical tradition that you personally follow. It is very important that you contemplate not only the teachings concerning each element, but the associated symbols and images as well.

1. The Conditions of Entrance
2. The Reception
3. Ecclesiastes 12:1-7
4. The Circumambulations

29. The Anchor and the Ark
30. The Forty-Seventh Problem of Euclid
31. The Hour Glass
32. The Scythe
33. The Spade
34. The Setting Maul
35. The Coffin
36. The Grave
37. The Sprig of Acacia
38. Travel in Foreign Countries
39. Master's Wages

In developing your understanding of each of these elements, you are advised to use all four types of contemplation – associative, analytical, intuitive, and interactive – within the context of the centering exercise. You may also use the Secret Smile as the technique leading to associative, analytical, or intuitive contemplation, though not for interactive contemplation. It is recommended that you practice the interactive form no more than twice per week. Altogether, each element of the previous list should be worked on for at least a few days, completing no more than two per week. Depth of understanding for each element is always more important than the speed with which you advance to the next. Indeed, you will find that many elements continue to reveal their depths over years of contemplation. Be patient and use your best judgment before moving from one element to the next.

To begin a session of interactive contemplation, perform the centering exercise. When you reach the step for contemplation, formulate a single question concerning some part of the ritual and symbolism of the Master Mason degree that you want to understand more fully. Next, imagine yourself clothed in a white robe, wearing your apron as a Master Mason. Visualize yourself standing at the closed outer door of a lodge room. Knock upon the door, listening to the knock reverberating into the depths of the Cosmos. You hear the knock returned, and the door opens to reveal a Master Masons' lodge at labor with the four officers at their stations. Note the illuminated symbol above King Solomon. Step inside and close the door behind you. Advance to the altar, notice its arrangement, present yourself in due form, and see King Solomon respond in kind. At this time you should invoke the aid of Deity with a short, heartfelt prayer asking for more light.

After your prayer, advance by the north to the east and approach King Solomon, the Worshipful Master. Note the illuminated symbol above his head. Ask him your question, keeping in mind that if he responds it will be with the voice of your spirit. As a Master Mason, more emphasis is placed upon intuition and the balance of intellect, emotion, and behavior. Therefore, you may spend more time in the east, asking further questions of King Solomon. When you are ready, thank him and continue clockwise to the south.

Approach Hiram Abif and ask him your question. You should also inform him about any response you were given by King Solomon. His answers may be characterized by reason and balanced judgment. You may also ask a few questions to gain greater clarity and understanding of what he is communicating. When you are ready, thank him and continue clockwise to the west.

Approach King Hiram of Tyre and ask him your question. You should also inform him of what happened in the east and in the south. His responses may be emotional in nature, expressing strong desires and convictions about the issue. You may ask him questions about why he feels the way he does. When you are ready, thank him and continue clockwise to the north.

Approach the Senior Deacon and ask your question. You should also recount what transpired in the east, south and west. This officer's responses may be focused on the physical world, with instruction on ways to physically experience or express the truth of what you are learning. Because of the change in priorities with this degree, you need not spend as much time with the Senior Deacon. When you are ready, offer your thanks and return directly to the altar.

At the altar, note the arrangement of the Three Great Lights. You should then express your gratitude with a short, heartfelt prayer of thankfulness. After the prayer, excuse yourself in due form, seeing King Solomon respond accordingly. Once again take note of the illuminated symbol above his head. Walk to the outer door, open it, and pass through. Turn to face it as it you close it. Allow the imagery to fade and complete the last steps of the centering exercise. Make appropriate notes in your journal.

"The 'secrets' of Freemasonry and of initiation are largely connected with this process of introversion of the soul to its own Centre, and beyond this brief reference to the subject it is inexpedient here to say more." — W.L. Wilmshurst, *The Meaning of Masonry*

MARROW IN THE BONE

Whereas the Entered Apprentice degree placed emphasis on behavior and emotions, and the Fellow Craft on the mind, the Master Mason's task is to realize an integration of the spirit as fully as possible. This is not always an easy task, for the spirit is elusive, fleeing from our grasp yet always present. In this section, you will be introduced to a technique that can help you establish better contact with the spirit, recognizing it as the mysterious yet undeniable essence of your being.

In the Master Mason ritual, we see that the body of Hiram Abif has very quickly putrefied in the grave. The skin slips from the flesh and the flesh from the bone, but the marrow in the bone has remained, making it possible to raise the body by the special grip of a Master Mason. There are many meanings to be found in this allegory, but for now, let us relate it to the levels of the psyche and our search for the core reality of our being.

For human beings bound to this mortal existence, the realization of "I am" is immediately apparent, yet accompanied by a strange uncertainty. It begs the question: "What am I?" Given the limitations of our awareness and understanding, this question may seem no less profound than inquiring about the nature of God. Many of us respond to this question with words like "spirit" or "soul." Yet when we are pressed to explain these terms, most of us have nothing but statements of faith or quotations from scripture to support our claim.

Despite the elusive nature of the spirit, the great traditions of spiritual enlightenment consistently assert that it is a real dimension of being. In fact, spirit is often considered most real. Furthermore, it is held that spirit can be experienced directly and does not have to remain a vague abstraction or a mere belief. As a contemplative Mason, you will use the following method to seek direct experience of the spirit.

EXERCISE 3:4

Perform this exercise once a day for two weeks. Begin by performing the centering exercise. When you reach the place for contemplation, take the following steps, which have been presented as a script. You may use this script to make an audio recording to guide you through the exercise. At the pauses, allow a minute or two for reflection. Stop using the recording when you are able to move easily through each step.

1. Say to yourself, "I am. What am I? Am I my body?" In your imagination, examine the physical dimension of your being in detail. Note its complexity and the intricacy of its design. (Pause) Note its extensive powers of sensation and movement. (Pause) Note the significance of the statement, "I have a body," and that while the body is a part of your being, it is not the "I" that says, "I am." (Pause) Say to yourself, "I am not my senses, my movements, my bodily processes." (Pause)

2. Say to yourself, "I am. What am I? Am I my emotions?" (Pause) Examine the emotional dimension of your being in detail. Note its richness and infinite variety. (Pause) Note its powers of desire, attraction and repulsion. (Pause) Note the significance of the statement, "I have emotions," and that while the emotions are a part of your being, they are not the "I" that says, "I am." (Pause) Say to yourself, "I am not my feelings, my desires, or my passions." (Pause)

3. Say to yourself, "I am. What am I? Am I my mind?" Examine the mental dimension of your being in detail. Note its broad expanse and freedom. (Pause) Note its powers of memory, imagination, analysis, and synthesis. (Pause) Note the significance of the statement, "I have a mind," and that while the mind is a part of your being, even that part in which these statements are heard and understood, it is not the "I" that causes the mind to say and hear "I am." (Pause) Say to yourself, "I am not my memories, my imagination, or my thoughts." (Pause)

4. Say to yourself, "I am. What am I?" (After a long pause for silent contemplation, complete the last steps of the centering exercise.)

It is not possible to describe what you might experience in the fourth step of this contemplation. It may be that nothing particularly meaningful or revealing ever occurs to you as a result of this work. On the other hand, it is possible that you may experience the most meaningful and revelatory event of your life. Between these extremes, you are likely to simply experience an inquisitive openness that waits to be filled or a quiet moment of knowing that transcends the thought of "I am." Whatever it is, however you experience it, it will happen in the way that is most appropriate for you.

To find the Absolute in the Infinite, in the Indefinite, and in the Finite, this is the Magnum Opus, the Great Work of the Sages, which Hermes called the Work of the Sun. — Albert Pike, Morals and Dogma

TO SEEK A MASTER'S WAGES

Every Master Mason claims that the third degree was sought in order to travel in foreign countries, and there, to work and seek a Master's wages, which would better enable the fulfillment of one's duties to self, family, and fraternity. Ironically, however, the symbolic significance of that work and those wages is never explained to the new Master Mason. As a contemplative Mason, you are encouraged to seek a deeper level of understanding and practice. In this section of the book, a specific interpretation will be offered for your consideration, as well as a very powerful tool in your continuing work as a contemplative Mason.

If we do not take the statement regarding travel in foreign countries literally, then what can it mean? Simply put, it must mean that by pursuing a level of mastery in our Craft, we will pass through territories that are unfamiliar to us. As a candidate in Masonic rituals, you experienced movement through strange events, emblems, and words which only later gained any depth of meaning for you. As a contemplative Mason, you have taken that work even further to explore unfamiliar regions of your mind and spirit. That travel is not yet done, nor will it be, so long as the silver cord is not loosed and the golden bowl is not broken.

In these travels, we say that we are seeking a Master's wages. As Speculative Masons, we know that there is a moral and fraternal aspect to this symbolism. No one who lives by the tenets of Masonry could fail to gain respect and support from others, and that is indeed a great commodity. Still, we should not assume that this is the last ray of Masonic light on the subject. Rather, looking deeper into Masonry itself, we may recall that we have consistently attested that light is the thing we seek. Furthermore, upon being raised, we were charged to discover the Lost Word of Masonry, which was lost when Hiram Abif was slain. Might these treasures, light and the Lost Word, be the greatest wages for a Master Mason?

As a contemplative Mason working the exercises of this book, you know that you have received further light and that there is always more light to be experienced. However, we have not yet addressed the issue of the Lost Word. If you have taken the so-called "higher" degrees of Masonry, then you have certainly been exposed to at least one notion of what the Lost Word may be. In fact, there are degrees professing to have the Lost Word in a certain form, only to have other forms provided in later degrees within the same rite! What are we to make of this cacophony of "Lost Words?"

It is the position of this book that the Lost Word is indeed the deepest and most profound mystery of the Masonic art, as well as the greatest wage of a Master Mason. It is also asserted that the Master Mason's ritual holds a key to the Lost Word. According to the most common forms of that ritual, the three assassins of Hiram Abif are Jubela, Jubelo, and Jubelum. Any competent Masonic scholar can tell you that, with the exception of Jubela, there are no such names in the Holy Bible or in the Hebrew language. There are similar names, such as the brothers Jabel, Jubel, and Tubal, but these are not used in the ritual. Therefore we must conclude one of two things about the names that have become standardized; either the writers of the ritual willingly used names that were utterly nonsensical, or they chose names that were intended to draw our attention to a great Masonic secret.

Whether intentionally so or not, the names of the ruffians conceal and reveal an ancient word. This book is not the first to point out that the suffixes of the three ruffians names are A, O, and UM. Likewise, it is not a new revelation that the sounds of these letters combine to produce the Sanskrit *Aum*, which learned Masons of the 18th century surely would have recognized.

It is important to note that we are not claiming Aum is the Lost Word. Instead, we assert that it is a *key* to the Lost Word, a key much like that which King Solomon thought might be found on or near the body of Hiram Abif. Of course, this point leads to more questions. If the word hidden within the Master's degree is not the Lost Word, but a key to the Lost Word, then how is it used to unlock that mystery?

There is very profound significance in Aum, especially for contemplatives. According to Vedic philosophers, the three basic sounds in the unity of Aum represent the deepest mysteries of being. Three categories of consciousness are associated with its sounds: AH is said to refer to the state of wakefulness; OH is said to refer to the state of dreaming; and MM refers to the state of dreamless sleep. Similarly, the three letters correspond to three attributes of the Divine – Creator, Preserver, and Destroyer. Most importantly, it is said that meditation upon this word has the power to enlighten the mind and to free one from illusion and the fear of death.

If we follow the Vedic teaching about Aum, then we should use it in meditation as a key to unlock the very mysteries of being and consciousness. Those mysteries are symbolized by the phrase, *the Lost Word*. In Masonry and other traditions, the Lost Word is often said to be the *Ineffable Name of God*, that name which cannot be spoken in sound or thought. It is not possible to speak the Lost Word or Ineffable Name because it is not possible for us to comprehend the Ultimate Truth, much less speak it. However, the ancient wisdom traditions of the world resoundingly declare that this Ultimate Truth can be *directly experienced*. For example, in Psalms it is written, "Be still and know that I am God." Jesus said to his followers, "The kingdom of God is within you." In this context, such passages suggest that the Lost Word is not a word at all, but the potential realization of one's spiritual communion with the Divine.

In the following exercise, you will use this key in a special meditation. It is important to understand that this meditation probably will not result in a lightning flash of ecstatic revelation. Although such an event is possible, expecting it is likely to lead to frustration and despair when it does not occur. Actually, the most significant power of this meditation is not in its potential to open the heavens or take you away from this world. Rather, the most significant power is in its potential to open your consciousness to the presence of the Divine Light right here and now, manifesting in ways that might otherwise seem too ordinary to fully appreciate. You are therefore encouraged to practice this meditation as an act of devotion; it is an expression of your commitment to seek the light of Masonry and the Lost Word. The more you practice, the more it can help you become an instrument of light in all that you do.

Rest assured that this practice will have positive benefits in your life. It has been repeatedly demonstrated that the regular practice of such meditation brings a deeper and more abiding sense of serenity, as well as sharper intuition and intellectual abilities. Furthermore, significant physiological benefits are quite common, including reduced blood pressure and an improved immune system. Clearly, such wages can enable you to better serve yourself, your family, and your fraternity.

EXERCISE 3:5

Practice this exercise each day for two weeks. Begin with the centering exercise. When you reach the step for contemplation, bring to mind the word Aum. Take a full breath and as you exhale, fill your mind and body with the silent intoning of that word. Feel each of its sounds as you silently draw the word out across the entire exhalation, "AAAOOOUUUMMM." With your next exhalation, slowly, smoothly, and deeply chant the word aloud, "AAAOOOUUUMMM." Feel the vibrations of the word throughout your body. As you repeat the word, allow your attention to focus on the center of your forehead. Feel the vibrations strongly in that spot. Begin to visualize the All Seeing Eye as the center of those vibrations. Continue to chant the word, allowing the vibrations to make a shift in your consciousness. At some point, after several repetitions, stop chanting the word aloud. Repeat it silently in your mind a few more times and feel the vibrations shifting to the top of your head, becoming subtler. Imagine a brilliant sphere, a Blazing Star, of purest white light hovering just above your head as the center of those vibrations. As the image becomes clear in your mind, allow its energy to radiate down through your body. Experiencing the bliss of that energy, removing your concentration from the image and the word, allowing yourself to merge with and dissolve into that light. Allow yourself to simply slip into the experience itself, without any expectations whatsoever. Whatever happens, let it happen. Just *experience* this part of the meditation rather than *doing* it. Make no attempt to control the experience in any way. Now is the time to relax very deeply, releasing yourself into pure, simple awareness. At some point, you will decide that it is time to end the meditation. At that point, focus your attention on your breath as you inhale and exhale in a natural rhythm. After a few breaths, complete the centering exercise in the usual manner.

"Love is ever the Builder, and those who have done most to establish the City of God on earth have been the men who loved their fellow men. Once let this spirit prevail, and the wrangling sects will be lost in a great league of those who love in the service of those who suffer. No man will then revile the faith in which his neighbor finds help for today and hope for the morrow; pity will smite him mute, and love will teach him that God is found in many ways, by those who seek him with honest hearts." — Joseph Fort Newton, *The Builders*

SPREADING THE CEMENT

As Master Masons, we learn that our special working tool is the trowel, an instrument actually used to spread cement, but which Speculative Masons use for the more noble and glorious purpose of spreading the cement of brotherly love and affection. While we are taught this cement should unite us as a harmonious and productive fraternity, it is important to understand that such is not its only application. The Master Mason should wield the trowel everywhere, at all times, and with all people. Love is so central to our Craft that we repeatedly find it touched upon throughout our degrees.

In effect, the lesson of the trowel brings us full-circle to rediscover the very thing that made it possible for us to enter the lodge as candidates, as well as the most important teachings of the First Degree. Consider, for example, the principle tenets – truth, relief, and brotherly love – and the third rung of the Entered Apprentice's ladder, which is the virtue of charity. While brotherly love, *philia* to the Greeks, obviously relates to the present theme, we can further discern that Relief does as well. What is relief if not the caring and compassionate effort to reduce or eliminate the burden of another? The special virtue of relief is that it is not merely a fraternal sentiment, but love in action. In fact, relief of a distressed worthy brother is so noble that it is even accorded to the same section of the 24-inch gauge as the service of God! Likewise, the traditional explanation of truth is not merely an intellectual abstraction; instead, it is an exhortation to replace hypocrisy and deceit with sincerity and forthrightness in both our hearts and words, and thereby promote our mutual welfare and rejoice in each other's wellbeing. As with brotherly love, charity clearly connects with love; indeed, the Latin source of this word, *caritas*, and its Greek counterpart *agape*, specifically refer to a selfless, unconditional, and generous love, or universal benevolence.

This kind of love is sometimes called "spiritual love." Beyond these examples, it would be worthwhile to review all the virtues inculcated in Masonry and meditate upon how each is best understood in the context of love. Love is at once the prime motive force, the most desirable sentiment, the most admirable action, and the worthiest product of our work as Masons.

The work of this section is developed through four phases. The first phase should be practiced for at least a week, and then each phase can be successively added over a period of several weeks until you are finally practicing all four phases in each sitting. Once a working familiarity has been developed with each phase, then you may place more or less emphasis on various phases, and even rearrange them as desired. Some people might find this method suitable as the main-stay of their regular devotionals and inner work, while others might prefer to use it less routinely. This method is an excellent practice for anyone who wishes to serve in spiritual healing, for it helps in keeping one's soul open to the flow of higher energies and tends to infuse one's healing prayers with the special sweetness of selfless love.

EXERCISE 3:6

Begin by offering a prayer of submission to the Divine Will, expressing your desire to know and serve it through love. Call to mind the image of someone you consider to be a great historical embodiment and exemplar of love. For instance, a Buddhist might think of Guanyin, a Christian of Jesus, or a Hindu of Parvati. Imagine this person standing in front of you with a loving smile. See within his or her chest a flaming heart, radiating love out through the whole body in rich hues of pink, ruby, and golden light, like a splendid sunrise. Feel the warmth on your face and chest. Let yourself respond emotionally to this great figure of love, smiling in return. Imagine your exemplar reaching out to cup your heart in his or her hands, and the flames of love flowing into and igniting your own heart. If you feel moved to weep with gratitude or smile or laugh with joy, allow that to happen as you continue to meditate upon this person as an embodiment of Divine Love, a living vessel through which God loves the world, including you. To accept this love is itself an act of love for God, for the exemplar, and for yourself. You may speak with your exemplar if you wish.

In your meditation, consider that to ancient people the heart was not merely symbolic of emotions, but was also the seat of intuition, inspiration, beauty, peace, and harmony. There is much to discover here about the nature of love, which includes far more than our feelings of affection and sympathy, and actually subsumes and transcends all dimensions of our being.

When you are ready to end the meditation, simply let the image fade. Offer a final prayer of thanks and return your consciousness to the external world, now infused with an elevated awareness of love.

While most people report this exercise to be positive and uplifting, some people may also find themselves challenged by various kinds of discomfort with the work. For example, feelings of unworthiness, guilt, or shame may arise. It is important to simply be aware of all our feelings, both pleasing and uncomfortable, accepting them as indicators of deeper processes occurring within our hearts and minds. In effect, they present us with opportunities to learn more of what we really believe about ourselves and our relationships with the Divine. In response to such observations, it is important to remember that accepting Divine Love is not about using the head to strategize a path toward righteous worthiness, but is rather about simply opening the heart to the immediate fact of God's mercy and affection. With this understanding, where we find self-condemning thoughts and feelings of self-loathing, we have the opportunity to practice acceptance, forgiveness, and healing of our own humanity, as well as truly nurturing ourselves toward more virtuous living.

EXERCISE 3:7

Proceed through the previous exercise and just past the point where your heart is ignited by the exemplar. Allow the image of the exemplar to fade, and in its place imagine someone among your friends and family with whom you share a deep bond of love. Perhaps this is someone you know to be in extra need of receiving love at this time. See him or her smiling in the warmth of the pink, ruby, and golden light radiating out through your body. Imagine yourself reaching forward to hold that person's heart in your hands. See and feel the flames of your heart flowing through your arms to ignite his or her heart with love. Speak with this person if you wish.

Meditate upon the love you have shared, how it has been expressed between you, and how it might grow.

When you are ready, allow that person's image to fade. If you feel moved to do so, allow the image of another cherished friend or family member to arise and then repeat the entire process. You can continue through as many loved ones as you wish, eventually ending the meditation as before.

As with the previous phase, this can be a very touching and joyful exercise, and yet it can also prove challenging. In focusing on your love for another, you might discover areas of uncertainty or sense something lacking. For example, you might realize that in some way you have not been as expressive of your love and affection as you might be. This could be due to various fears or inhibitions for either or both of you. You might also discover that you have resentments, frustrations, or other negative feelings about the individual that seem to prevent you from more fully and freely loving him or her. As you practice the exercise with different people in mind, you may become more aware of how your love differs from one person to another. With some people, these sentiments might be more affectionate, with others, more appreciative or admiring, while for still others, more compassionate or sympathetic. In any case, this phase of spreading the cement of love can help you learn about how you feel, think, and behave in your relationships with loved ones, and thus provide you with many opportunities to refine your ability to love each person in your life in a way as unique and meaningful as he or she is.

EXERCISE 3:8

Work through the first two phases, and now begin extending your love toward someone you feel has mistreated or offended you in some way or someone you have difficulty trusting. Give just as freely and energetically to this soul as you did in the second phase. Meditate upon the many pearls of wisdom in loving those we may not find easy to love. Reflect on what it means to love someone you do not necessarily like. Ponder how you might manifest love for this person more outwardly. As before, repeat the process until you are ready to end the meditation.

EXERCISE 3:9

After working through all the previous phases, meditate upon the universe as existing within the Flaming Heart of God. Recall that your heart is aflame with that same Divine Fire and think of it as a spark of that Divine Fire, as are the hearts of all God's children. Allow all the implications of meaning, virtue, and action to flow freely through your heart and mind, with neither resistance nor attachment, but with awareness, acceptance, and love.

The solitary, private practice of this method has great potential to nurture your awareness and understanding of love. For those who believe in the power of prayer, it will be no stretch of the imagination to hope for it having beneficial effects beyond oneself. Yet as contemplative Masons, we should not be content to limit our labors only to the inner lodge of our hearts and minds, but we should also actively engage them in the material and social world. For love to be whole and healthy, it must be expressed in our deeds and experienced in our relationships with others. Therefore, you are urged to regard this method as a source of inspiration and insight, that you may more masterfully wield the trowel in every aspect of your life.

The essence of oneself and the essence of the world: these two are one. Hence separateness, withdrawal, is no longer necessary. Wherever the hero may wander, whatever he may do, he is ever in the presence of his own essence – for he has the perfected eye to see. There is no separateness. Thus, just as the way of social participation may lead in the end to a realization of the All in the individual, so that of exile brings the hero to the Self in all. — Joseph Campbell, The Hero With a Thousand Faces

FROM LABOR TO REFRESHMENT, ON TO LABOR AGAIN

After having practiced the previous two exercises, you have followed the course of this book up the hierarchy of the psyche, from the physical to the spiritual. Taking these most recent exercises as the pinnacle of our work, one might think that the ultimate goal of contemplative Masonry is simply to revel in such highly spiritual states of consciousness. However, this notion is far from the truth. One of Masonry's first lessons is that we are to divide our time equally among three important aspects of life: service of God and our fellow members, our usual vocations, and our need for refreshment and sleep. This lesson is only one example of a repeating theme of balance and harmony in the Craft. In the final exercises of this book, you are reminded to observe such order, ordained in Nature, as a routine part of your life.

When you received the Master Mason's degree, you were charged to emulate the integrity of Hiram Abif. This lesson refers not only to his honor and commitment to principles, but also to a state of union in his internal and external qualities, one in which all parts were fitted with exact nicety. In fact, the word *integrity* has the same root as the word *integrated*, revealing our deep awareness of the importance of such order and harmony. It is time to apply this wisdom to the levels of the psyche, for up to now we have seen them as somewhat distinctly different means of experience and expression.

Although it is useful to understand the psyche in terms of a hierarchy, it is also useful to think of it as a unified whole. If you have sincerely delved into the work of this book, then you surely have already seen that the physical, emotional, mental, and spiritual aspects of our being are constantly operating in relation to each other. In fact, it is often difficult to determine where one level ends and another begins. So now, rather than thinking of the psyche in terms of a ladder or stairway, let us think of it as a spoked cog in a craftsman's machine. In this model, each aspect of the psyche is dependent upon the others in order for the whole to function at all. Let us think of the spiritual aspect of the psyche as represented by the drive shaft, the center upon which the cog must rotate smoothly. The intellect is the hub, keeping the cog in proper alignment. The emotional aspect is the set of spokes transferring the energies manifesting within the cog, both the forces driving it to work for the craftsman and the forces of resistance it encounters from other systems. The physical aspect is the set of teeth on the cog, engaging other systems and producing movement in its environment. For the psyche, like the cog, the whole is no stronger than its weakest part; there must be a proper balance among its elements.

Our challenge is to fine-tune ourselves as living cogs in the grand machinery of the universe. To be sure, you have already engaged that work in significant ways. When you reached the final lesson of mindful and prayerful behavior, you practiced simultaneous awareness of each level. It is hoped that you work to establish that as an ongoing aspect of your life. As another example, each time you practice the interactive contemplation technique, you have established a working harmony between spirit, mind, emotion, and body. In the following exercises, you will build upon that foundation using the interactive form of contemplation as well as two final techniques for holistic maturation.

EXERCISE 3:10

The description of this exercise is simple. You use the interactive form of contemplation as you did for the ritual and symbols of the Master Mason degree. However, you are now advised to use this method for a broader range of purposes: working out the solution to any problem; seeking deeper insight into any teaching, symbol or relationship you may encounter; or looking deeper within yourself for understanding of your own spirit, thoughts, feelings, and behavior. As you perform this technique, remember that it is important to report at each station what has transpired at the previous stations.

EXERCISE 3:11

This exercise is used for the same purposes as the previous, but may require less time and energy. Begin by forming a short statement expressing the issue under consideration. Perform the Secret Smile. When you reach the step for contemplation, examine the issue from a purely physical point of view. Note the various sensations you experience and behaviors you enact that are associated with this issue. At some point, take a full breath and as you exhale, begin to consider the issue from a purely emotional perspective. Allow yourself to feel the various desires, emotions, and passions associated with the issue. At some point, take a full breath and as you exhale, begin to consider the issue from a purely intellectual point of view. Do a thorough rational analysis of thoughts, images and judgment concerning this issue. At some point, take a full breath and as you exhale, begin to clear your mind and make an opening for intuition. Simply sit quietly in intuitive contemplation. To finish the contemplation, take another full breath and as you exhale, begin to put all the pieces together into a harmonious relationship. When you are ready, complete the Secret Smile and make notes in your journal.

EXERCISE 3:12

This exercise may require even less time than the previous. Begin by forming a short statement expressing the issue under consideration. Perform the Secret Smile. When you reach the step for contemplation, ask yourself how the issue would look from a perspective of superhuman power. Allow yourself to feel a sense of incredible power. At some point, take a full breath and as you exhale, ask yourself how the issue would look from the perspective of perfect compassion. Allow yourself to feel deeply loving. At some point, take a full breath and as you exhale, ask yourself how the issue would look from a position of transcendent wisdom. Allow yourself to feel profoundly wise. To finish the contemplation, take another full breath and as you exhale, begin to put all the pieces together into a harmonious relationship. When you are ready, complete the Secret Smile and make notes in your journal.

CONCLUSION

The duties of the Junior Warden include calling us from labor to refreshment and on to labor again. So it should be with your contemplative work. The time you spend in peaceful contemplation of the spirit may seem to you to be a blissful respite from the struggles of everyday life. Be careful in this respect, for many have started down the contemplative path only to be tempted into escapism and denial of their role as an instrument of light in the world. You are encouraged to develop a routine of contemplative work that addresses each dimension of your being, uniting them into a wiser, more beautiful, and stronger whole. *Appendix A: On a Contemplative Routine* offers suggestions about which techniques to continue practicing, as well as recommendations on how often to practice.

In closing, it is sincerely hoped that you have found this book to be a valuable collection of tools. If so, please share those tools with other members of our Craft. There are far too many who feel called to contemplative Masonry for us to keep this work a closely guarded secret. It is time that we encourage one another and make known throughout our fraternity that such work is not merely acceptable, but necessary in order to produce the fullest benefits of our art.

Adieu! A heart-warm fond adieu,
Dear brothers of the mystic tie,
Ye favored, ye enlightened few,
Companions of my social joy.

Robert Burns, *"The Farewell," 1786*

APPENDICES

APPENDIX A: ON A CONTEMPLATIVE ROUTINE

The following list presents a summary of each technique that is recommended for ongoing work. To the right of each is a suggestion regarding a minimal inclusion in a contemplative lifestyle. It is assumed that most persons attempting to establish such a routine will have the typical 40-hour work week with a need for family time and social interaction, such as attending lodge. Under such circumstances, it can sometimes seem quite difficult to fit contemplative work into your schedule, but remember that something small is better than nothing at all. Therefore, keep in mind that these are only recommendations, and you should exercise appropriate judgment in developing a schedule for yourself.

Exercise	Frequency of Practice
1:8 – Deep, cleansing breathing	each morning
1:9 – Deeply relaxed breathing	each night
2:4 – The Secret Smile	once daily
3:5 – Meditation on Aum	thrice weekly
3:9 – All four phases of Spreading the Cement	once weekly
3:11 – Integrated contemplation within Secret Smile	once weekly

Exercise	Frequency of Practice
3:12 – Wisdom, compassion, and power contemplation	once weekly
1:21 – Transformative contemplation of vices and virtues	once monthly
3:4 – "I am. What am I?"	once monthly
3:10 – Interactive contemplation of Master Mason	once monthly
1:5 – Attendance of Masonic functions with emphasis on mindfulness of all levels	at every Masonic function
1:1 – Attendance of Masonic functions with emphasis on mindfulness of the physical	as needed
1:2 – Attendance of Masonic functions with emphasis on mindfulness of the emotional	as needed
1:3 – Attendance of Masonic functions with emphasis on mindfulness of the mental	as needed
1:4 – Attendance of Masonic functions with emphasis on mindfulness of the spirit	as needed
1:15 – The Centering Exercise	as needed

Exercise	Frequency of Practice
1:19 – Bodily contemplation of opposing emotions	as needed
1:20 – Transformative contemplation of opposing emotions	as needed
Dreamwork	as needed
Study of Science and Spirituality	as needed

Please note that some of these techniques can be combined in a single session. For example, 3:11 or 3:12 can immediately follow 3:5. Likewise, 2:4 can immediately follow 1:8 or 1:9. For exercises with a daily, monthly, or weekly schedule, it is suggested that you set routine days and times for each. Any technique may now be used as often as needed. However, those specifically marked "as needed" should be used whenever one feels a lack of awareness or understanding in the relevant areas of life or levels of the psyche. The basic centering exercise, 1:15, should be used whenever you want to perform a purely associative, analytical, or intuitive contemplation. Finally, remember that mindful and prayerful behavior has been recommended as an ever-present way of life.

APPENDIX B: BIBLIOGRAPHY

(Note: Many of the older books listed here present histories of Masonry that we now know to be largely speculative and factually incorrect. They nonetheless remain useful for their insightful treatment of Masonic symbolism and philosophy.)

ON MASONRY

- *The Beginning of Masonry*, by Frank C. Higgins
- *The Builders*, by Joseph Fort Newton
- *Building Cement: Uncommonly Concrete Masonic Education*, by John S. Nagy
- *Duncan's Ritual of Freemasonry*, by Malcom C. Duncan
- *Encyclopedia of Freemasonry*, by Albert Mackey
- *Esoteric Freemasonry*, edited by Isaac Maier
- *Freemasonry: A Journey through Ritual and Symbol*, by W. Kirk MacNulty
- *Freemasonry: Its Hidden Meaning*, by George H. Steinmetz
- *Lightfoot's Manual of the Lodge*, by Jewel P. Lightfoot
- *The Lost Keys of Freemasonry*, by Manly P. Hall
- *The Masonic Myth: Unlocking the Truth About the Symbols, the Secret Rites, and the History of Freemasonry*, by Jay Kinney

- *A Masonic Thought for Each Day of the Year*, by Alphonse Cerza
- *Masonry and Its Symbols, in the Light of Thinking and Destiny*, by H.W. Percival
- *The Masons Words: The History and Evolution of American Masonic Ritual*, by Robert G. Davis
- *The Meaning of Masonry*, by W.L. Wilmshurst
- *Morals and Dogma of the A.A.S.R.*, by Albert Pike
- *Mystic Masonry or the Symbols of Freemasonry and the Greater Mysteries of Antiquity*, by J.D. Buck
- *Some Deeper Aspects of Masonic Symbolism*, by A.E. Waite
- *Stellar Theology and Masonic Astronomy*, by Robert Hewitt Brown

ON SCIENCE AND SPIRITUAL PSYCHOLOGY

- *Anatomy of the Soul*, by Edward Edinger
- *Archetypal Psychology: A Brief Account*, by James Hillman
- *The Ego and Dynamic Ground: A Transpersonal Theory of Human Development*, by Michael Washburn
- *The God Theory: Universes, Zero-point Fields, and What's Behind It All*, by Bernard Haisch
- *History and Systems of Psychology*, by James Brennan
- *Integral Psychology*, by Ken Wilber
- *Jung: A Very Short Introduction*, by Anthony Stevens

- *Jungian Archetypes: Jung, Gödel and the History of Archetypes*, by Brian Robertson
- *Motivation and Personality*, by Abraham Maslow
- *Mysticism, Mind, Consciousness*, by Robert Forman
- *The Portable Jung*, edited by Joseph Campbell
- *Psychosynthesis: A Psychology of the Spirit*, by John Firman and Ann Gila
- *Sacred Geometry: Philosophy and Practice*, by Robert Lawlor
- *The Science of Oneness: A Worldview for the Twenty-First Century*, by Malcom Hollick
- *Taking the Quantum Leap: The New Physics for Non-scientists*, by Fred Alan Wolf
- *Wholeness and the Implicate Order*, by David Bohm

ON ESOTERICISM, MYTHOLOGY, PHILOSOPHY, AND RELIGION

- *Access to Western Esotericism*, by Antoine Faivre
- *Anthology of World Scriptures*, by Robert E. Van Voorst
- *The Hero with a Thousand Faces*, by Joseph Campbell
- *Hidden Wisdom: A Guide to the Western Inner Traditions*, by Jay Kinney and Richard Smoley
- *The Inner West: An Introduction to the Hidden Wisdom of the West*, edited by Jay Kinney
- *Magic and the Western Mind: Ancient Knowledge and the Transformation of Consciousness*, by Gareth Knight
- *Mysticism and Philosophy*, by William Stace

- *Oneness: Great Principles Shared by all Religions*, by Jeffrey Moses
- *The Secret Teachings of All Ages: An Encyclopedic Outline of Masonic, Hermetic, Qabbalistic and Rosicrucian Symbolical Philosophy, Being an Interpretation of the Secret Teachings concealed within the Rituals, Allegories and Mysteries of All Ages*, by Manly P. Hall
- *Western Esotericism and Rituals of Initiation*, by Henrik Bogdan
- *The World's Religions*, by Huston Smith

ON MEDITATIVE PRACTICES

- *Centering Prayer and Inner Awakening*, by Cynthia Bourgeault (Christianity)
- *Gate to the Heart: A Manual of Contemplative Jewish Practice*, by Zalman Schachter-Shalomi (Judaism)
- *Kundalini Awakening: A Gentle Guide to Chakra Activation and Spiritual Growth*, by John Selby (Vedanta)
- *The Middle Pillar*, by Israel Regardie (Hermeticism)
- *Mindfulness in Plain English*, by Bhante Gunaratana (Buddhism)
- *Seeing with the Mind's Eye*, by Samuels and Samuels (Secular/Eclectic)
- *Sufi Meditation*, by Lex Hixon (Islam)
- *Taoist Ways to Transform Stress into Vitality: The Inner Smile Six Healing Sounds*, by Mantak Chia (Taoism)

ABOUT THE AUTHOR

Chuck Dunning has been a Master Mason since 1988, is a member of Blue Lodges and Scottish Rite Valleys in both Texas and Oklahoma, and also belongs to a number of Masonic research societies. In the Scottish Rite, Chuck is a Knight Commander of the Court of Honor, Director of Education for the Guthrie Valley in Oklahoma, and a Class Director for the Fort Worth Valley in Texas. In 2012 he became the founding Superintendent of the Academy of Reflection, which is a chartered organization for Scottish Rite

Masons wanting to integrate contemplative practice with their Masonic experience.

Chuck has been engaged in various forms of contemplative practice for over three decades. In his career in higher education and mental health, in Masonry, and with other groups and individuals, he facilitates and teaches mindfulness, meditation, and imagery to enhance their experiences of life in many ways. Chuck holds a master's degree in counselor education and a bachelor's degree in psychology, both from the University of North Texas.

Anyone interested in contacting Chuck about speaking engagements or contemplative workshops may do so at:

chuck@thelaudablepursuit.com

Made in the USA
Middletown, DE
12 December 2017